Making Dimensional Wood Plaques

Making Dimensional Wood Plaques

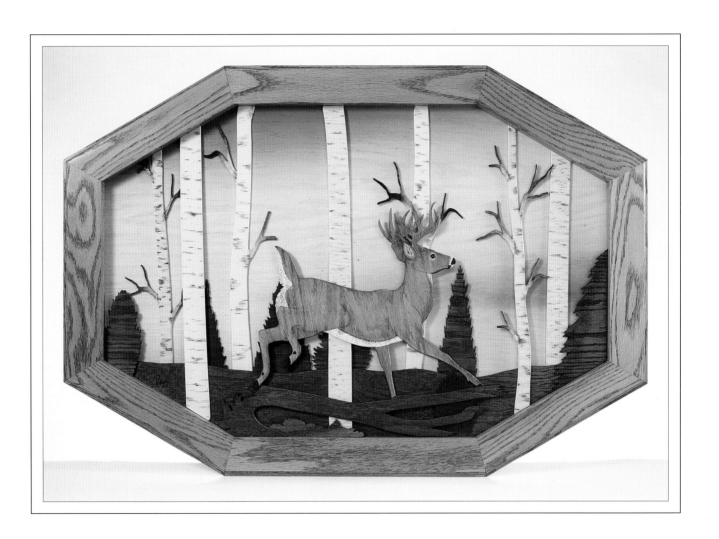

Patrick Spielman
& Robert Hyde

Sterling Publishing Co., Inc. New York
A Sterling/Chapelle Book

Chapelle, Ltd.:

Jo Packham
Sara Toliver
Cindy Stoeckl

Editor: Kelly Ashkettle
Art Directors: Karla Haberstich,
Mackenzie Johnson
Copy Editor: Marilyn Goff
Graphic Illustrator: Kim Taylor
Staff: Areta Bingham, Donna Chambers,
Emily Frandsen, Lana Hall, Susan Jorgensen,
Jennifer Luman, Melissa Maynard,
Barbara Milburn, Lecia Monsen,
Suzy Skadburg, Linda Venditti,
Desirée Wybrow

Cover and finished project photography:
Barry Stahl, Ovation, Inc., La Crosse, WI

Library of Congress Cataloging-in-Publication Data

Spielman, Patrick E.
  Making dimensional wood plaques / Patrick Spielman & Robert Hyde.
    p. cm.
  ISBN 1-4027-0692-8
  1. Jig saws. 2. Woodwork--Patterns. I. Hyde, Robert. II. Title.
TT186 .S6656 2004
684'.08--dc22   2003025172

10 9 8 7 6 5 4 3 2 1

Published by Sterling Publishing Co., Inc.
387 Park Avenue South, New York, NY 10016
©2004 by Patrick Spielman and Robert Hyde
Distributed in Canada by Sterling Publishing
c/o Canadian Manda Group, One Atlantic Avenue, Suite 105
Toronto, Ontario, Canada M6K 3E7
Distributed in Great Britain by
Chrysalis Books Group PLC, The Chrysalis Building,
Bramley Road, London W10 6SP, England
Distributed in Australia by Capricorn Link (Australia) Pty. Ltd.
P. O. Box 704, Windsor, NSW 2756, Australia
Printed and Bound in China
All Rights Reserved

Sterling ISBN 1-4027-0692-8

Every effort has been made to ensure that all information in this book is accurate. However, due to differing conditions, tools, and individual skills, the publisher cannot be responsible for any injuries, losses, and/or other damages which may result from the use of the information in this book.

This volume is meant to stimulate woodcrafting ideas. If readers are unfamiliar or not proficient in a skill necessary to attempt a project, we urge that they refer to an instructional book specifically addressing the required technique.

Due to limited space, we must print our patterns at a reduced size in order to give our patrons the maximum number of patterns possible in our publications. We believe the quality and quantity of our patterns will compensate for any inconvenience this may cause.

If you have any questions or comments, please contact:

Chapelle, Ltd., Inc.
P.O. Box 9252
Ogden, UT 84409
(801) 621-2777
(801) 621-2788 Fax
e-mail: chapelle@chapelleltd.com
web site: www.chapelleltd.com

CONTENTS

Acknowledgments

We express our thanks and appreciation to our typist Jennifer Blahnik and to our assistant woodworker Dan Jahnke.

We also wish to acknowledge our spouses, Patricia Spielman and Carole Hyde, for their steadfast support and helpful assistance.

Acknowledgments by Robert Hyde

When a hobby turns into a full-time occupation, it can be overwhelming. I was lucky that my wife Carole was able to devote both her time and creative skills to what became our business. As our workload grew, my friend Daniel Jahnke was able to take on the production of all the frames that I needed.

I was again lucky a few years later when a high school acquaintance built a home near me. His three bright and energetic children worked with us for several years. Without the help of Greg, Jeff, and Stacy Heezen we would have been unable to keep up with the workload. Last but not least is Irene Treadway (Carole's aunt) who helped with coloring and detail work, and in many other ways.

INTRODUCTION

The beautiful pieces of wall art in this book are the exclusive creations of scroll-saw artist and coauthor Robert Hyde. The projects are selected from the best-sellers of Mr. Hyde's numerous wooden pictorials, developed over a 20-year period of making and marketing more than 10,000 of these compelling designs.

Layered wall art involves three areas of work: making frames; making and coloring the backgrounds; and making, coloring, and mounting the layered cutouts. (See Fig. i-1.)

Fig. i-1: Layered, colored, and mounted wall art.

In the following pages, Mr. Hyde provides the original patterns and reveals his techniques, tips, and shortcuts so anyone can make these appealing wall hangings. Permission is hereby granted to produce unlimited quantities not only for personal enjoyment, but for resale as well.

The 20 projects in this book effectively combine several areas of woodcrafting, including simple frame joinery, scroll-sawing, wood-burning,

finishing, and assembly. The techniques are easy to learn. The projects essentially consist of individually scroll-sawn and painted cutouts from ⅛"-thick plywood that are systematically arranged in as many as six layers within a frame to create stunning dimensionality. (See Fig. i-2.)

Fig. i-2: Layered cutouts of ⅛"-thick plywood.

The finished works appear more detailed and complex to make than they actually are. Most projects are easily completed using acrylic paints, marking pens and a coloring system that is almost as fundamental as "painting by numbers." The tools and materials necessary to get started are primarily a scroll saw, a flap sander mounted onto a used motor, a narrow belt sander, and a wood-burning tool. These are readily available and need not be expensive. In fact, Robert's initial power tool investment was less than $150 for the economy grade of bench-top tools which he still uses today. (See Fig. i-3 on page 8.)

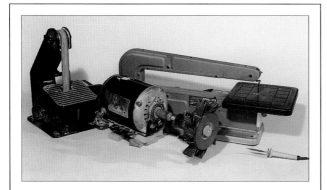

Fig. i-3: Primary tools used to produce the pictures.

You may already possess the necessary tools and skills. Once involved in this fascinating work, you may wish to embellish the designs by creating them in various sizes; substituting different materials, colors, or framing designs, or infusing other ideas to give these projects your own distinguishing style.

Most of the pieces in this book are made from multiple layers of ⅛"-thick oak plywood, stained or painted to obtain attractive colors. Bright coloring of small areas is done quickly using felt-tip markers. (See Fig. i-4.)

Fig. i-4: Small, brightly colored areas.

Larger pieces are colored with a "wash" of acrylic paint and water, which allows the wood grain to show. A variety of different woods in their natural or augmented colors could be substituted. (See Fig. i-5.)

Fig. i-5: Layered outdoor scene.

However you elect to use the patterns and information in this book, you have before you some of the most luxurious designs available for the discriminating scroll-sawyer. They are designed to allow you to deliver projects with the most visual impact and with the least amount of effort. It will be difficult to find any other scroll-sawing activity that will provide more pride and satisfaction or be more dazzling to friends, family, or customers.

— Patrick Spielman, 2004

Chapter 1
Making the Frames

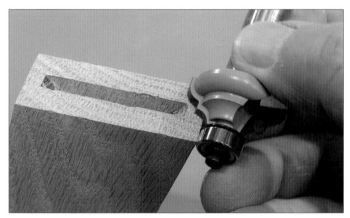

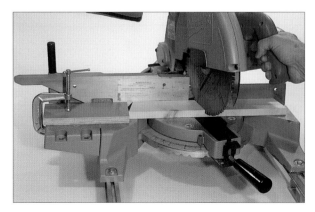

Most works of art are framed after completion. Creating layered scroll-saw art, however, requires fitting some pieces against the inside edges of the frame as the work progresses. (See Fig. 1-1, below, and refer to Fig. i-2 on page 7.)

Fig. 1-1: Finished in realistic colors.

Each project consists of a ¾" or thicker solid wood frame, a one-piece or a segmented plywood background, and up to six layers of ⅛"-thick plywood cutouts finished in realistic colors. Techniques for making special frames designed for this purpose are discussed in this chapter. Purchased wood moldings and framing stock of various sizes and shapes may also be used.

The section drawing shows how the background is attached behind the frame and how many of the layered pieces butt against the inside edge.

Note: The background is not considered one of the layers within the frame. (See Fig. 1-2.)

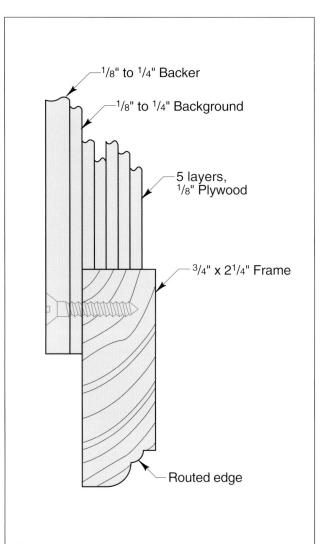

¹/₈" to ¹/₄" Backer

¹/₈" to ¹/₄" Background

5 layers, ⅛" Plywood

³/₄" x 2¹/₄" Frame

Routed edge

Fig. 1-2: Section drawing shows how the background and backer are attached behind the frame and the thin layered pieces are built up inside the frame.

Making the Frames. All of the frames illustrated in this book are made of red oak, but other woods may be used. Red oak is easily obtained and it stains well.

Projects that consist of five or more layers of ⅛"-thick plywood require a framing stock that is surfaced to a minimum of ¾" thickness. If it is available, ¹³/₁₆"–⅞"-thick wood is a better choice for the five- or six-layer projects. Projects with five or fewer layers will be framed nicely using standard stock of ¹¹/₁₆"–¾"-thick material.

Frame Styles. The frames are categorized by their overall shape. These are: square, rectangular, round, and oval. The recommended width of the frame stock is 2¼", but it may vary plus or minus ⅛". The outside lengths, however, should be cut as specified. (See Figs. 1-3, below, and 1-4 on page 12.) Any changes made to the frame will require changes to the backer, background, and fitting of the "inside" layers. Insure that all of the frame pieces are as uniform as possible in color and figure. Prepare the wood to uniform width and thickness, favoring a finished thickness of ¾" or more. Miter the ends according to the lengths and angles specified.

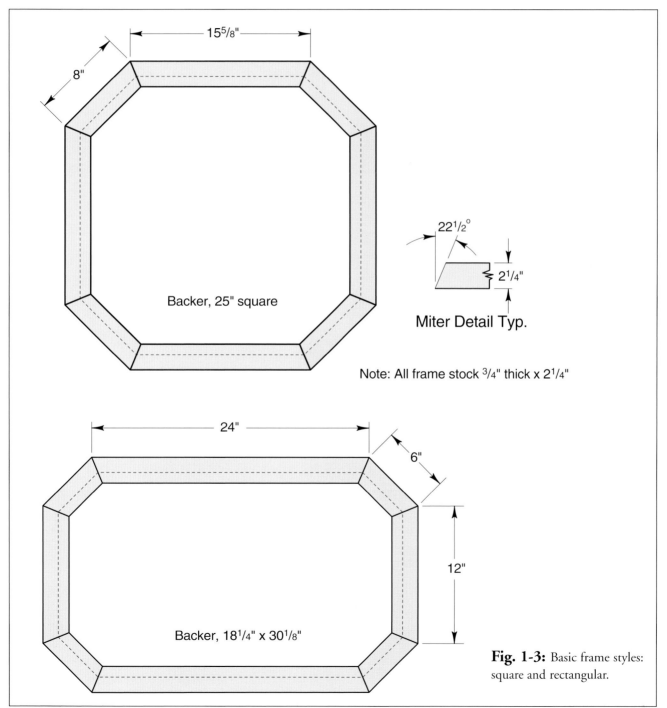

Backer, 25" square

15⁵/₈"

8"

22¹/₂°

2¹/₄"

Miter Detail Typ.

Note: All frame stock ³/₄" thick x 2¹/₄"

24"

6"

12"

Backer, 18¹/₄" x 30¹/₈"

Fig. 1-3: Basic frame styles: square and rectangular.

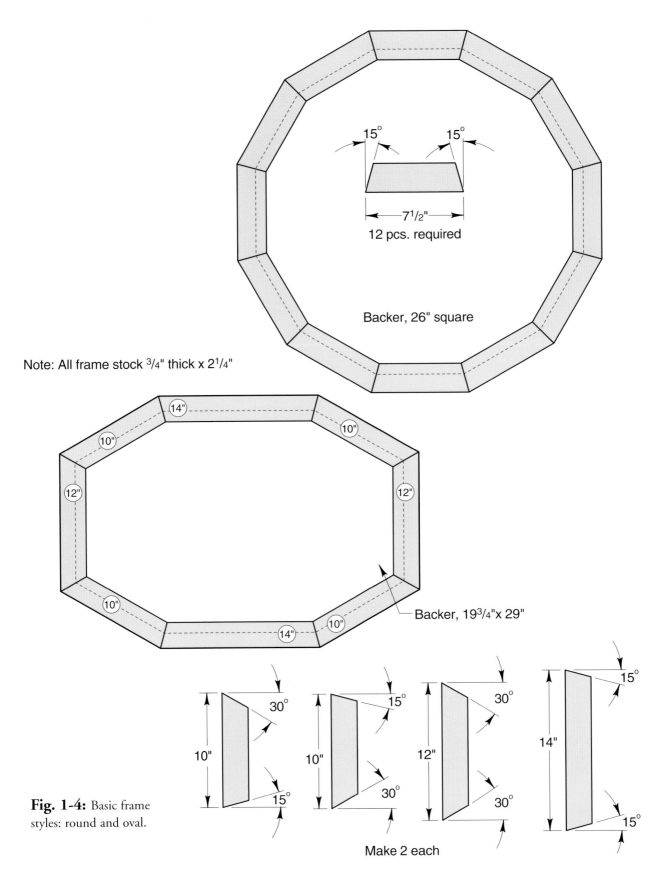

15°   15°

7¹/₂"

12 pcs. required

Backer, 26" square

Note: All frame stock ³/₄" thick x 2¹/₄"

14"

10"   10"

12"   12"

10"   10"

14"   10"

Backer, 19³/₄"x 29"

30°   15°   30°   15°

10"   10"   12"   14"

15°   30°   30°   15°

Fig. 1-4: Basic frame styles: round and oval.

Make 2 each

Cut a test piece on a power miter saw. Check angles and lengths. For making identical lengths, use a power miter saw or a table saw with stops. (See Fig. 1-5.)

Fig. 1-5: Plywood stop clamped to saw table to insure identical lengths.

Tip: First make test cuts from inexpensive wood to test the saw setup.

Check the cuts with a large square. Assure that the cut surfaces will be vertical. (See Fig. 1-6.)

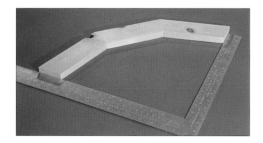

Fig. 1-6: Three practice pieces, comprising ¼ of a round frame.

Once the pieces have been cut to size, make a dry-run assembly using a ratchet-type band clamp and no glue to assure that the angles are cut perfectly. (See Fig. 1-7.)

Fig. 1-7: A test assembly with a band clamp.

Next, incorporate a suitable method to strengthen the glued joints. This may be as simple as exposed finishing nails or concealed framing biscuits or splines that fit into prepared slots. The recommended way to strengthen joints is to use biscuitlike splines scroll-sawn from solid wood with the grain running perpendicular across the joint. Be certain that the edge-decorating bit to be used later will not cut into the slots. (See Figs. 1-8 and 1-9, and Fig. 1-10 on page 14.)

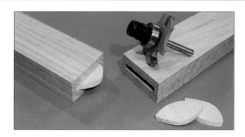

Fig. 1-8: Slot cutter, one of several kinds and sizes.

Fig. 1-9: Ample room for edge-decorating bit.

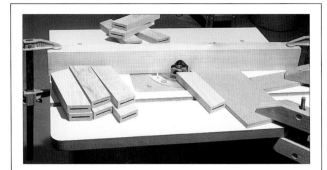

Fig. 1-10: Router table set up for cutting slots.

With all machining, fitting, and checking complete, make the final glued assembly. (Refer to Fig. 1-7 on page 13.) An extra set of hands to assist with glue spreading (or nailing) and handling the band clamp will be helpful.

After the glue has cured, clean off excess glue and sand all surfaces until level before machining the outside edges. (See Figs. 1-11 through 1-14.)

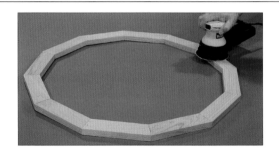

Fig. 1-11: Cleaning up glue and sanding all joints and surfaces.

Fig. 1-12: Decorative edge options: routed profiles (top), sawn bevel (bottom).

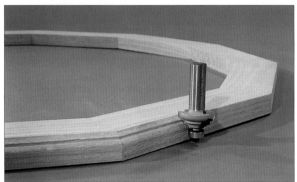

Figs. 1-13 and 1-14: Decorative edge-routing with a hand-held router or a router/shaper table.

Apply a suitable stain, such as medium oak or walnut, that is neither too light nor too dark. A clear protective topcoat will be applied later, as the final step, after all layers have been cut, colored, and assembled. (See Fig. 1-15.)

Fig. 1-15: Stain the frame as desired.

CHAPTER 2
MAKING THE BACKGROUNDS AND BACKERS

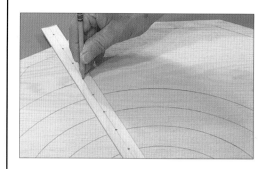

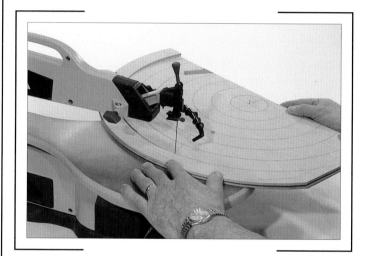

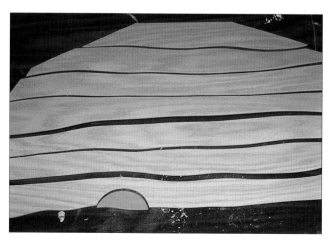

One-piece Backgrounds. Backgrounds are exposed on one side to the viewer and the various cut-out layers and/or shims are glued onto the background. Backgrounds are made from ⅛"- or ¼"-thick plywood; and they are made as either a one-piece painted background or as one that is cut into irregular segments. Most of the background and layer pieces for the projects in this book were made from ¹⁄₁₀"- or ⅛"-thick red-oak plywood. Painted backgrounds do not require a backer. (See Figs. 2-1 and 2-2.)

Fig. 2-2: The Gathering project: segmented background, finished by adding progressively greater amounts of blue acrylic to a whitewash.

Segmented Backgrounds. The segmented backgrounds are stained or painted, then glued onto another piece of uncut low-quality plywood called a "backer." (See Figs. 2-3 and 2-4, and refer to Fig. 1-2 on page 10.)

Fig. 2-1: The Cattail project: one-piece plywood background with horizontal grain, colored with acrylic whitewash (paint and water).

Fig. 2-3: Red-oak plywood for layers and backers.

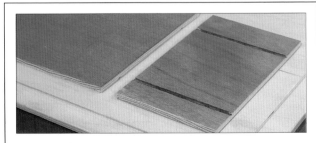

Fig. 2-4: Both surfaces of recycled wall-paneling, which makes an economical backer material. (The finished surface on the right, glueable back surface on the left).

16

The outside shapes of the backgrounds correspond to the basic shapes of the frames. Backgrounds and backers are about 1" larger all around than the inside opening of the frame.

There are five basic segmented background styles used on the projects in this book. (See Fig. 2-5, and Figs. 2-6 through 2-9 on pages 18–21.)

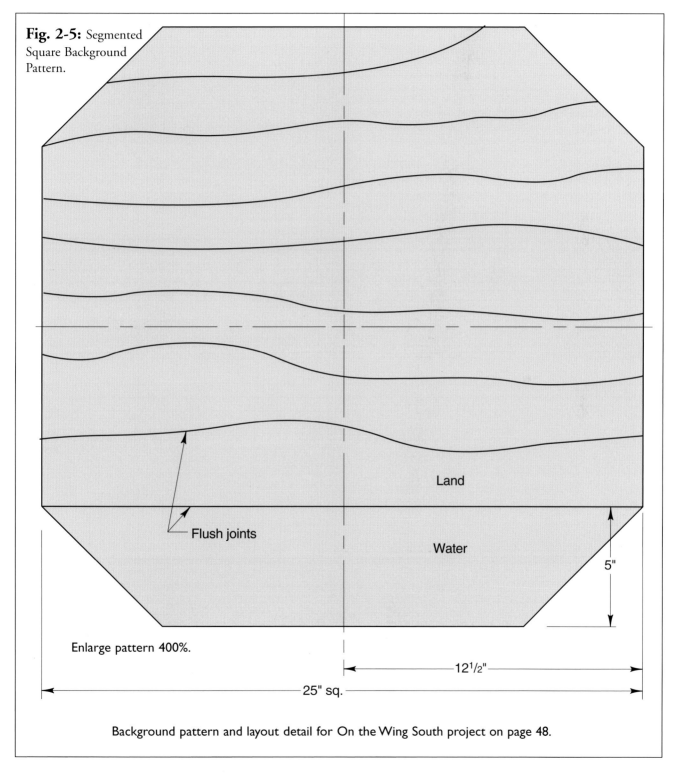

Fig. 2-5: Segmented Square Background Pattern.

Land

Water

5"

Flush joints

Enlarge pattern 400%.

12¹/₂"

25" sq.

Background pattern and layout detail for On the Wing South project on page 48.

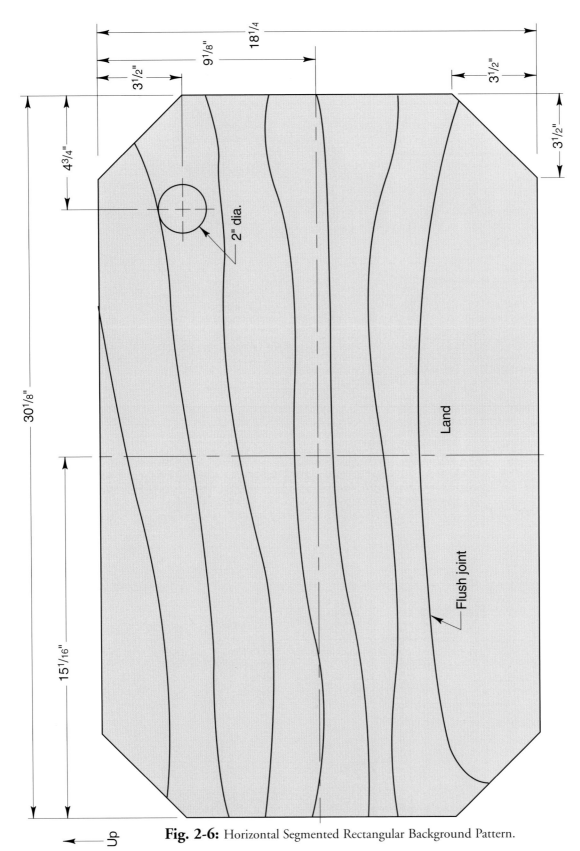

Fig. 2-6: Horizontal Segmented Rectangular Background Pattern.

Background pattern and layout detail for The Gathering project on page 70.

Enlarge pattern 400%.

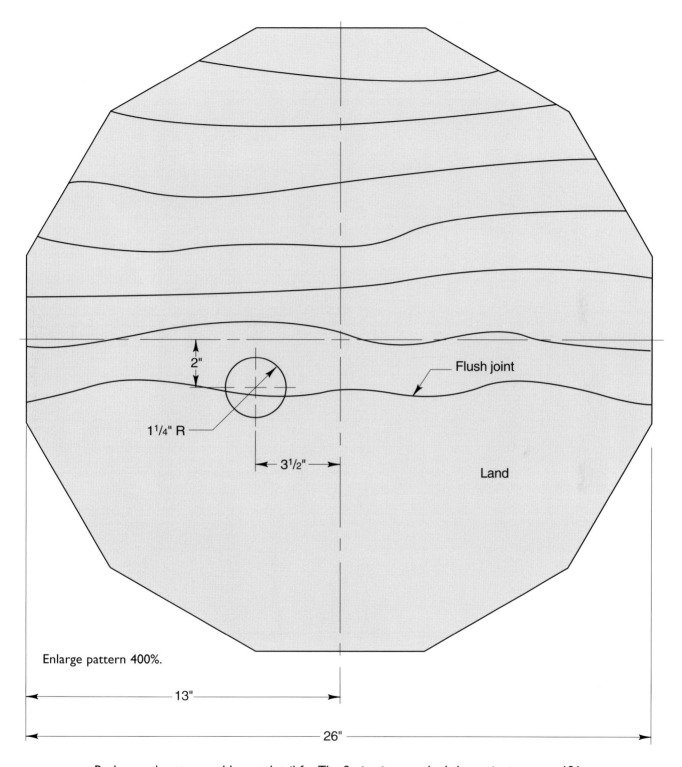

2"

Flush joint

1¹/₄" R

3¹/₂"

Land

Enlarge pattern 400%.

13"

26"

Background pattern and layout detail for The Springtime on the Lake project on page 131.

Fig. 2-7: Round Segmented Background Pattern.

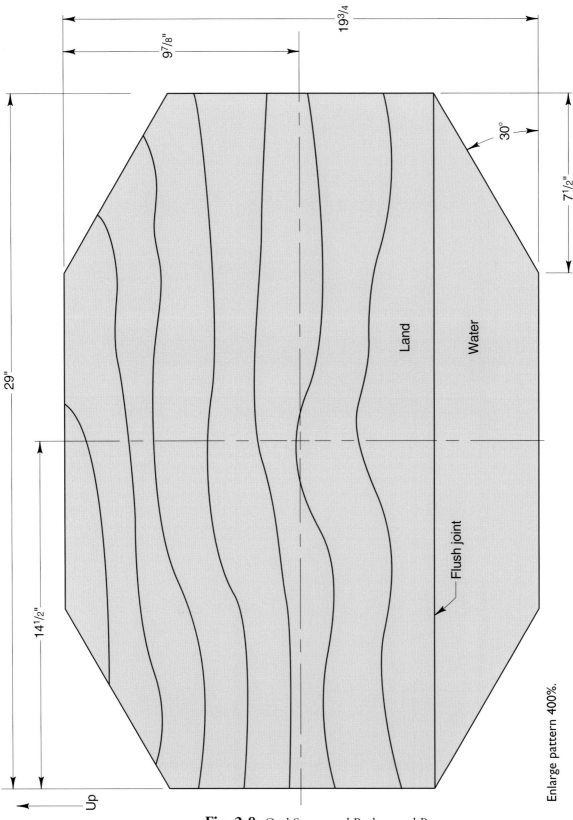

Fig. 2-8: Oval Segmented Background Pattern.

19³/₄

9⁷/₈"

30°

7¹/₂"

29"

14¹/₂"

Up

Land

Water

Flush joint

Background pattern and layout detail for The Two Bumps on a Log project on page 145.

Enlarge pattern 400%.

20

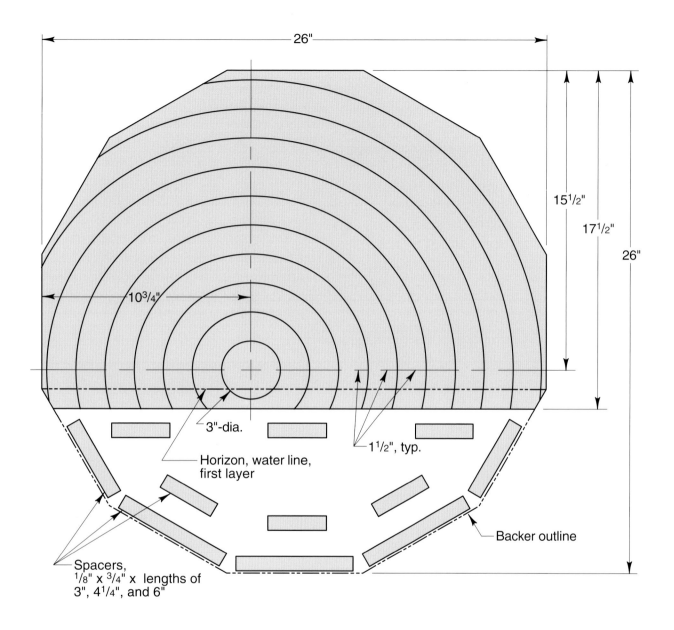

Background layout details for Monterey Sunset on page 63.
Note: For illustrative purposes, this drawing is not in scale.

Fig. 2-9: Compass-drawn layout and pattern for segmented round background of concentric circles.

Selecting the Background Wood. There are several variables that affect the final look of the one-piece and the segmented backgrounds and the various layer pieces such as land and water. Firstly, the grain pattern or figure of the wood itself can have a major effect. The range of different natural colors and grain patterns of rotary-cut plywood available can be quite extensive. Choose open-figured wood to simulate waves of water and wispy cloud formations. The face grain of the plywood is essentially either "rotary cut" or "sliced." This refers to the two methods of cutting face veneers from the log. Sliced veneers have a much finer texture and straighter lines. Pay attention to grain quality. (See Fig. 2-10.)

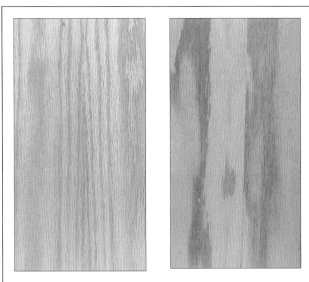

Fig. 2-10: Various natural colors and grain patterns.

Avoid seams when possible because they detract from the natural look. Secondly, the type of finish obviously influences the final look of your project. Yellow reds can simulate a sunset, whereas a white-gray paint will represent dusk and the like. The intensity of the colors applied can also affect the visual results. Dark colors and/or multiple coats can be employed to create a silhouetted look. It is entirely up to the taste and efforts of the individual artist.

Making Segmented Backgrounds. Laying out the irregular segmented cutting lines is, in most cases, best done freehand. The sample patterns shown in Figs. 2-5 through 2-8 on pages 17–20 require enlargement and the use of a photo copy machine. The layout for each background is somewhat different for every project.

Mark the top on the rear with an "up arrow" for future orientation when fitting various layers to the inside edges of the frame. Use the inside of the frame as a reference and lay out the outside cutting lines approximately 1" greater all around than the inside opening. (See Fig. 2-11, below, and Fig. 2-13 on page 23.)

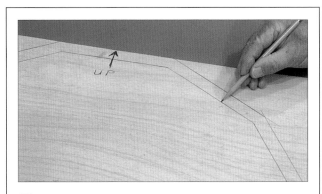

Fig. 2-11: Frame layout and cutting lines.

Refer to the project photos if you need some guidance, and note how the lines relate to the joint locations of the frame, using them as reference points. By and large, the layouts for segmented backgrounds shown in this book were determined by the grain patterns of the particular piece of plywood used.

Divide the sky area into as many irregular horizontal pieces as you wish, with 5–9 pieces being a good range.

The background for the Monterey Sunset project on page 63, however, has specifically spaced concentric circles which must be compass-drawn. Lay out segmented concentric circles, using a strip of wood with a series of pencil-hole spacing 1½" apart. (See Fig. 2-12, below, and refer to Fig. 2-9 on page 21.)

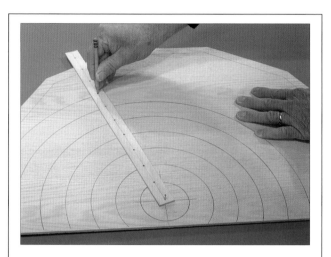

Fig. 2-12: Compass-drawn concentric circles.

Sawing Segmented Backgrounds. Usually a more artistic background effect can be achieved by making the irregular curved segmentation cuts freehand more or less following the grain or the natural figure lines of the wood. (See Fig. 2-13, below, and refer to Figs. 2-10 and 2-11 on page 22 and Fig. 2-2 on page 16.)

Fig. 2-13: Background cutting lines and layouts for larger landform layering pieces can be drawn freehand.

This work is best done with a variable-speed scroll saw or a band saw. Select either ⅛"- or ¼"-thick plywood for your particular background project. Almost any scroll saw that will carry plain-end blades is useable to make the projects in this book. (See Fig. 2-14).

Fig. 2-14: Scroll saw with plain-end blade.

Cut the outside profile and make the segmented cuts using a fine-skip-tooth blade in the No. 4–No. 6 size range. (See Fig. 2-15.)

Fig. 2-15: Left to right: No. 2 and No. 5 blades for fine work and a thick-wood blade useful for stack-sawing six or more identical pieces simultaneously.

The throat capacity of most scroll saws will not allow the background segment cuts to be made in one continuous pass. Cut inward to approximately halfway, pull the piece out, and begin the cut again from the opposite end.

An alternative way to make long cuts on the scroll saw is to twist the ends of the blade 90° so the cuts can be made band-saw fashion. Refer to Spielman's *New Scroll Saw Handbook* for this and other basic scroll-sawing techniques.

Cutting the segmented concentric circular background demands precise cutting skills. Since it is more difficult to control cuts in thin stock, add a sacrificial piece of waste paneling under the workpiece to provide additional feed resistance and better overall sawing control. (See Figs. 2-16 and 2-17, below, and refer to Fig. 2-13 on page 23.)

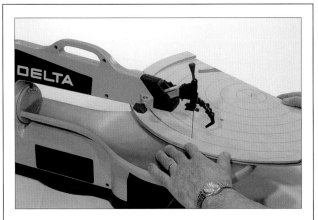

Fig. 2-16: Making perfect circular cuts in ⅛"-thick plywood is made easier with a slow blade speed.

The desired result is smooth, flowing curves of a true radius. (See Fig. 2-17.)

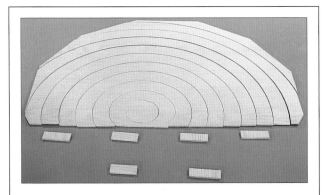

Fig. 2-17: The cut pieces and some of the spacers.

See the Monterey Sunset project on page 64 for more information and tips for finishing the concentric circle background. Shown below are two segmented backgrounds that are easier to cut with the scroll saw. (See Figs. 2-18 and 2-19.)

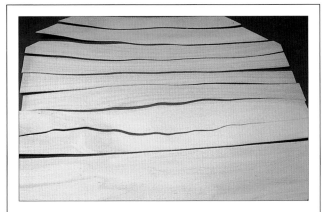

Fig. 2-18: Scroll-sawn segmented backgrounds ready for edge rounding over and color application.

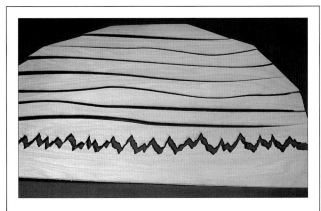

Fig. 2-19: If the layout is not cut perfectly, no one will ever know.

The edges of all segment pieces should be rounded over to a ¹⁄₁₆"–³⁄₃₂" radius. This can be done by hand, using a folded piece of 60- or 80-grit abrasive sandpaper. (See Fig. 2-20 on page 25.)

Fig. 2-20: Rounding over the mating edges of segmented background pieces.

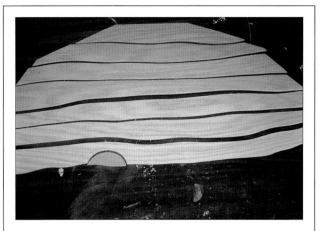

Fig. 2-22: Completed top portion of graduated-color background pieces changing from yellow gold to a bright red orange.

Coloring Background Segments. Generally, background coloring is done with acrylic paints. (See Fig. 2-21.)

Fig. 2-21: Acrylic paints, water, and paintbrushes.

Most are thinned with water to make a lightly pigmented "wash." When applied and immediately wiped off, the wood takes on just the right amount of color while still allowing the patterns of the wood to show through. Gradually increasing the amount of pigment as each adjoining segment is finished creates a dramatic graduated color scheme. (See Fig. 2-22.)

Beautiful sky backgrounds in graduated blue, white, and red-orange colors are surprisingly easy to create. Each successive piece will require a greater proportion of red pigment as you progress from the light-colored pieces to those with deeper tones. Test color mixture on pieces of scrap wood. Wipe off excess with paper toweling. (See Fig. 2-23, below, and Figs. 2-24 through 2-27 on page 26.)

Fig. 2-23: 10:90 mixture of yellow paint and water plus a small amount of red applied to first piece.

Fig. 2-24: Increased color intensity applied to second workpiece.

Fig. 2-25: Small amount of red acrylic paint added to mixture.

Fig. 2-26: Intensified red-tinted acrylic wash.

Fig. 2-27: Graduated results, similar to the background pieces shown in Fig. 2-22 on page 25.

Gluing Background Segments to a Backer.
Use any conventional woodworker's adhesive such as yellow carpenter's glue to adhere the background segments onto your backer piece. (See Fig. 2-28.)

Fig. 2-28: Flat strips of wood and cans containing sand or concrete provide clamping pressure.

Apply pressure to the glued flat surface.
Tip: It may be helpful to tack the first piece at the edges with brads to keep it from shifting as successive pieces are pushed tightly against each other.

Painting One-piece Backgrounds. Three projects feature one-piece backgrounds that are simply painted with a wash of white acrylic paint. Seven projects have white backgrounds painted with streaks of blue that blend softly into the surrounding whitewash. This sounds easy enough to achieve, but it is still best to practice on scrap before undertaking a full-sized background piece. The first step when painting a nonsegmented background is to apply whitewash. Allow to partially dry. White backgrounds are generously coated with a 50:50 mixture of water and white acrylic paint. (See Fig. 2-29.)

Fig. 2-29: Whitewashed nonsegmented background.

Use a dry brush to remove excess paint and brush marks. This will smooth and even out the coating. Allow it to set a few minutes, then wipe or brush off the excess to achieve the wash look so the grain is barely visible. If too much paint is removed, simply recoat and repeat the process until the desired look is attained. The entire painting process should take 10–15 minutes.

Painting White with Blue Streaks. Use three different paintbrushes for the following procedure. Use one brush for the whitewash and apply it as previously described. It is important to keep the whitewash wet so blending can occur in the next step. Using a smaller brush, apply the unthinned blue acrylic paint to two or three areas of the wet background. Let dry for two or three minutes. (See Fig. 2-30.)

Fig. 2-30: Random streaks of blue acrylic paint.

Finally, use a clean, dry brush and blend the edges of the blue paint into the white. (See Figs. 2-31 and 2-32.)

Fig. 2-31: Light blue transition areas.

Continue blending the edges of the blue, adjusting its intensity with the white area until the desired effect is achieved. Keep at least 75% of the background white. (See Fig. 2-32.)

Fig. 2-32: White and blue background.

Fitting Visible Layers Inside the Frame. Think ahead. Once the background is completed, use the inside of the frame to trace the edges of the various layered pieces that must fit perfectly against the inside edge of the frame. Pick those pieces out and concentrate only on cutting and fitting those areas or edges that will be visible in the finished project. Use a sharp pencil to trace the inside edges and angles of the frame onto those layering pieces that will be landforms or water. (See Fig. 2-33.)

Fig. 2-33: Fitting the layered pieces against the inside of the frame.

Sometimes only one corner or edge must fit perfectly. Be certain these are prepared to fit perfectly before attaching the background and backer (if required) to the frame. Sawing close to the layout line and finishing with a small hand plane works well. Remember to orient the fitting pieces to the same frame edge. Notice that the top of the frame is referenced with a piece of tape and the fitted piece will be visible only on the two edges indicated by the red arrows. (See Fig. 2-34.)

Fig. 2-34: Orienting fitted piece.

Fastening the Background to the Frame.
First, assure that the painted background is fairly smooth. The acrylic wash may raise the grain fibers. Use 400–600-grit sandpaper and hand-sand very lightly. Do not sand through the color. Orient the background correctly to the frame. Drill pilot holes for the wood screws to secure the background to the frame. (See Fig. 2-35.)

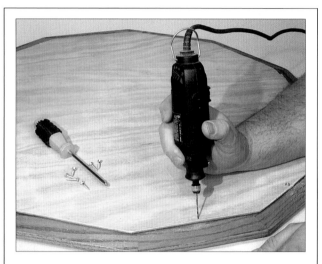

Fig. 2-35: Drilled pilot holes.

After all interior pieces are glued, anchor a wire between two of the screws for hanging. (See Fig. 2-36.)

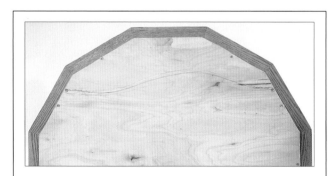

Fig. 2-36: Anchor wire.

CHAPTER 3
BASic LAYER Cutting and Coloring

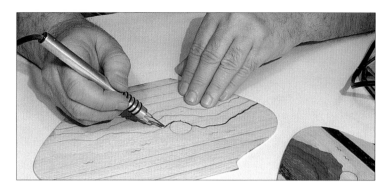

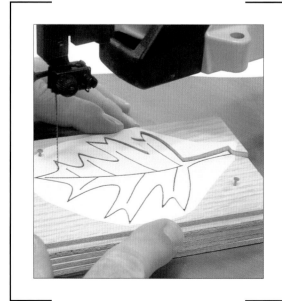

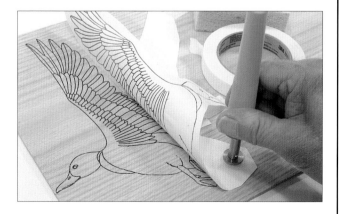

This chapter covers some basic techniques that apply to all of the projects. Also included here are instructions for creating the cattails that are found in five projects and instructions for creating the small geese which appear on the sky backgrounds in five projects. Tips for creating and coloring deer, which are featured in three projects, rounds out this chapter.

Patterns, Layout, and Cutting Layers. Enlarge and copy the patterns from this book onto paper or transparency film as necessary, using either a fine-point marker or a photocopy machine. Most photocopy machines distort enlarged copies somewhat, so some hand-corrections may be required where fitting is necessary. Transferring the pattern lines onto the wood for sawing and subsequent coloring can be done in either of the following ways: First, use carbon paper to transfer the enlarged pattern. (See Figs. 3-1 and 3-2.)

Fig. 3-1: Pattern copied on transparency film.

Fig. 3-2: Tracing with a fine-point marker.

The film can then be traced over carbon paper or used to make a reverse copy for use with the transfer tool. The transfer tool provides just the right amount of heat concentration to activate the toner delivered to the surface of the paper pattern with a photocopy machine. Depending upon the type of toner used, this technique may not work with computer printers. (See Fig. 3-3.)

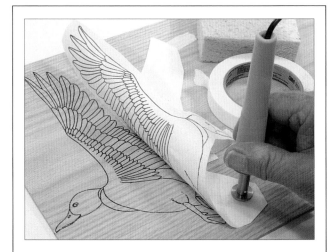

Fig. 3-3: Electrically heated transfer tool.

A regularly photocopied pattern will transfer onto the wood in a reverse position. That is, a bird facing right on the original pattern will be flipped and face left when transferred. This is where the transparency film comes into play. First, copy the pattern onto transparency film. (Refer to Fig. 3-2.) The transparency copy can then be flipped on the photocopy machine to make a reverse copy so that, when transferred, the pattern made on the wood will be facing in the right direction. Use ⅛"-thick plywood and check the grain direction when preparing pieces for cutting. (See Fig. 3-4.)

30

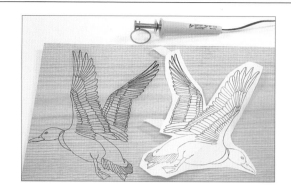

Fig. 3-4: Pattern transferred onto wood. Notice that the transferred copy is a reverse of the pattern.

Paper patterns of pieces with no interior wood-burning or coloring lines can be bonded directly onto the wood for scroll-sawing. Use a temporary bonding aerosol spray. (See Fig. 3-5.)

Fig. 3-5: Photocopied pattern temporarily bonded directly to wood.

Scroll saws with a variable-speed control are very helpful when sawing thin and small pieces. (See Fig. 3-6.)

Fig. 3-6: Auxiliary hardboard table with a small blade-entry hole is held in place with double-faced tape. This setup is ideal for sawing small parts and supporting fragile pieces.

A number of pieces may be stack-sawn all at the same time, using one pattern. Make identical parts by stack-sawing multiple pieces simultaneously. Layers can be held together with tape or tacked together with small brads in the waste area to hold the stack intact during sawing. (See Figs. 3-7 and 3-8.)

Fig. 3-7: Sawing tacked layers.

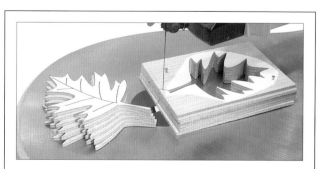

Fig. 3-8: Completed parts.

Tip: When nailing thin layers together for stack-sawing, set the workpieces on a flat steel plate, then drive the brads through the workpieces. The nails will peen themselves over, holding the bottom layer secure with no worry of nail points scratching the scroll-saw table.

Many of the cut-out pieces will look more realistic if the outside edges are rounded over. This can be done in the usual way by hand-sanding with a coarse-grit sandpaper, followed by finer grits to achieve smoothness.

Wood-burning Details and Coloring Lines.

Wood-burning is a key process because it creates detailed texturing such as feathering, and identifies or separates areas for coloring and/or staining with felt-tip markers and/or acrylic paints. Always continue burn lines over rounded edges on pieces that have them. (See Fig. 3-9.)

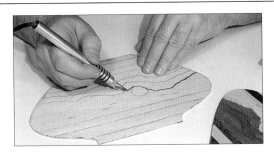

Fig. 3-9: Wood-burning detail lines.

Almost any wood-burning tool can be used. Better mid-priced units, however, offer adjustable electronic dial-controlled heat and power. They also have a wide selection of interchangeable tips that create very fine lines. If using a typical inexpensive "burning pen," file the end to a fine point. (See Fig. 3-10.)

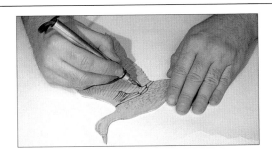

Fig. 3-10: Burning feather outlines on duck cutout.

Wood-burning detail lines helps to provide very sharp definition between adjoining colors and stains applied with felt-tip markers. The burned line acts as a dam, keeping the color dispensed by markers from bleeding across the line. This is clearly demonstrated when comparing a pencil line to a burned line's ability to contain bleeding. (See Fig. 3-11.)

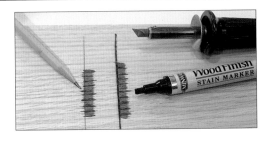

Fig. 3-11: Marker ink bleeding across the pencil line at left but not the burned line at right.

Finishing with Felt-tip Markers. (Refer to Fig. 3-11 and see Fig. 3-12.)

Fig. 3-12: Detailed coloring.

Markers are excellent for coloring and staining small areas of wood. They are available in a wide array of colors and many shades of stains. They come with various-sized tips ranging from an ultrafine point to a broad point that covers larger areas quickly. They can help achieve sharp definition without obliterating the natural figure of the wood. (See Figs. 3-13 and 3-14.)

Fig. 3-13: Staining with transparent brown marker.

Fig. 3-14: Notice how a second coating with a green marker around the outside edges increases the intensity of the color.

Almost any conventional line of markers sold in discount stores will work. Better markers and greater color selections can be found at art supply stores or through mail-order catalogs. Markers come with either felt or fiber tips, with the latter seemingly more durable on wood surfaces.

Tips: New markers are "juicier," in that they send more ink to the surface. When working two colors side by side, always put down the lighter color first. Thus, if there happens to be any bleeding across the line, the darker color will cover. Deeply burned lines, however, are best to keep colors contained in the intended areas.

Creating Cattails. Cattails are the focal point of Project No. 1 on page 40, and are secondary components in four other projects. Cattails can be made in two ways: by using built-up pieces of scroll-sawn plywood, or by using round dowels.

Plywood cattails are made from two layers of ⅛"-thick material. The internal cross-grain ply of the finely pointed ends tend to crumble when sawn. (See Fig. 3-15, below, and Figs. 3-16 and 3-17 on page 34.)

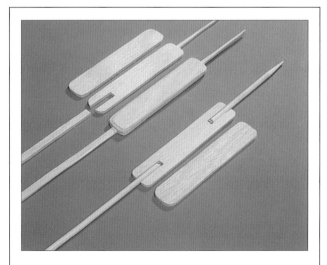

Fig. 3-15: Two-layer plywood cattails. Notice the rounded edges.

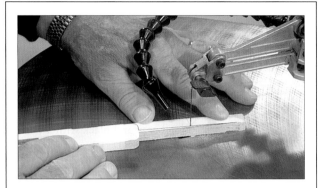

Fig. 3-16: Stack-cutting sharply pointed end, with two wraps of tape holding the layers together.

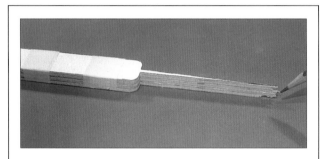

Fig. 3-17: Interior ply of the extremely brittle points.

The fine points are probably best dealt with by simply cutting off the last inch or so. Alternatively, you can strengthen the point by saturating the fragile tip area with glue after one side of it is sawn. Use a coarse-grit sandpaper and a sanding block to round over the edges of the upper piece and the edges of the stems and pointed ends.

Dowel Cattails. These look more dimensionally realistic; but they require a V-block jig and a drill press to make them properly. (See Fig. 3-18.)

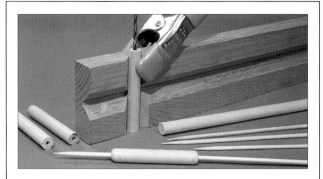

Fig. 3-18: A simple V-block, when set up on a drill press as shown, makes perfectly centered and straight holes into the dowel ends.

To make large dowel cattails, use ⅝"- or ¾"-diameter dowels, and ³⁄₁₆"- or ¼"-diameter dowels for the stems and points. Sharpen the dowels by rotating them against a power belt or disc sander. Flatten the cattail heads on one side of the larger dowels to provide a gluing surface.

Tip: Cut extra reeds and grasses that go with the cattails. This provides more flexibility and options during assembly. The grasses can be sawn off at their bottoms to adjust their heights.

Painting the Small Geese. Geese appear in five projects and require three colors of acrylic paints in separate containers and three small paintbrushes. Add a little water to make the paint easier to blend. (See Figs. 3-19, below, and Figs. 3-20 through 3-27 on pages 35–36.)

Fig. 3-19: Painted geese.

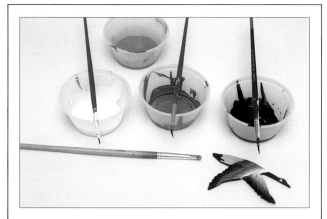

Fig. 3-20: Three containers of acrylic paint: black, gray (black and white mixed), and white. Notice the wide dry brush for blending in the foreground.

Fig. 3-23: Step 3: Blend gray and black with a wider dry brush.

Fig. 3-21: Step 1: Paint the black areas first.

Fig. 3-24: Add the white as shown.

Fig. 3-22: Step 2: Add some gray.

Fig. 3-25: Using another dry brush, blend white into gray and paint other areas white where needed.

Fig. 3-26 and 3-27: Completed geese.

Although these small geese are actually part of the first layer, it is best to glue them to the background after all other layers have been glued, so that they may be more artistically placed.

Making and Coloring Deer. When selecting the ⅛"-thick plywood for deer, it is generally recommended to avoid tight, vertically grained wood that can create a zebra look. It is also a good idea to cut all the deer in a project with similarly grained wood.

Cut out the deer, observing the direction of the grain. Be very careful when sawing the narrow tips of the antlers. Be certain to use an auxiliary saw table with a zero-clearance blade opening. (Refer to Fig. 3-6 on page 31.) This will support very small or delicate cuts over the table opening. Carefully round over all edges slightly.

General Coloring of Deer. Study Figs. 3-28 and 3-29 below, and Figs. 3-30 through 3-32 on page 37 for examples of partially-colored deer and close-ups of the coloring.

Tips: When coloring animals and birds, obtain some good color photos from books and magazines to use as a guide for coloring and shading. The instructions that follow pertain to the use of felt-tip marker colors that are applied after the wood-burned details are completed.

Fig. 3-28: Deer in various stages of completion. Left: Two deer with the first base coat applied. Bottom and right: Three small deer with darker areas shaded and blended into the base coat.

Fig. 3-29: Completely colored cut-out deer.

36

Fig. 3-30: Deer, sawn from vertical rotary-cut veneer plywood, totally finished.

Fig. 3-31: Closeup showing wood-burned detailing and marker-applied coloring.

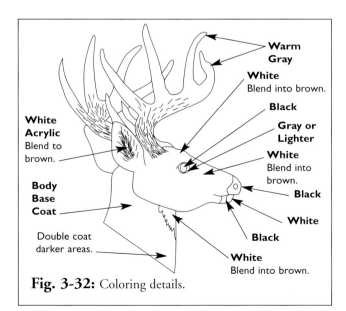

Warm Gray

White
Blend into brown.

Black

Gray or Lighter

White
Blend into brown.

Black

White

Black

White
Blend into brown.

White Acrylic
Blend to brown.

Body Base Coat

Double coat darker areas.

Fig. 3-32: Coloring details.

Marker colors labeled as "warm" contain red pigment which is good for deer tones. Colors labeled as "cool" have a bluish base and are not the best choice for coloring deer.

The base color for all deer should be a medium tan. (Refer to Fig. 3-28 on page 36.) At this point, do not color the antlers, hooves, nose, or the obvious white areas. The antlers are colored with a medium warm gray.

Shadows and Highlights. Always start with the lighter colors and then darken them as necessary. Attempt to simulate the shadows and highlights shown in the photos. Use a dark gray marker to make the darker shadow lines under the body, legs, etc. Keep a wet edge for blending colors. Next to the dark gray, add some medium gray and blend the two together. To achieve subtle darkening, recoat with the same marker color. Next, paint all white areas with acrylic. The hooves, nose, eye pupil, and chin areas are colored with a black marker. (Refer to Fig. 3-32.)

Ear Detail. The inner-ear area is painted with acrylic paint, blending the wet edges into the brown using a "blender marker"—a clear finish without any pigment. Apply a darker brown around the edge of the ear and use the blender marker to make the color transitions. Apply the blender marker to the wet acrylic, blending it into the brown/tan color. (Refer to Figs. 3-31 and 3-32.) Clean the blender tip frequently to remove any acrylic paint by rubbing it off while still wet.

Eye Detail. Use the same techniques employed for the ear. Paint white acrylic around the eye and blend with a blending marker into the brown. (Refer to Figs. 3-31 and 3-32 on page 37.) When the paint has dried, use an ultrafine-point permanent black marker to add the line details around the eye. This is somewhat like putting on cosmetic eyeliner to enhance eye details. Add black lashes and a dot of white in the upper left of the pupil to simulate the "glint" or flash of light.

Black and White Details. Apply white acrylic to the underside of the tail and belly, and use a black marker to color the hooves, nose, pupils, and shins.

Assembly of Layers. Along with the patterns for cutting and wood-burning pieces for the various layers, a sequential assembly plan is given layer by layer for each project. These give the approximate placement for each layer or level. Some parts are raised with small shim pieces positioned out of the viewer's sight. Particular instructions for such details are given with other specific instructions pertaining to each project.

Tip: After all pieces have been cut, fit, and colored, make a dry assembly to assure that all layers are artistically positioned.

Adhesives. Several types of glue can be used to adhere the various layered pieces onto the background. Although the strongest structural glue joints are made by gluing raw wood to raw wood, the authors have not experienced any glue failures using typical woodworker's adhesives on surfaces coated with acrylic paints or markers. It is, however, advised that the reader make his or her own tests, judgments, and determinations of the best performance for any particular types or brands of glue. It may be practical to use a combination of two types of glue on larger pieces. For example, use hot-melt or instant glue, which set quickly, to temporarily hold the piece in position while another glue applied to the same piece sets up. One of the disadvantages of hot-melt-type glues is the generally thick glue lines associated with their use. This may elevate the pieces

too much, resulting in raising the final layer(s) above the thickness of the frame.

Apply the glue ½"–¼" from the edge of the workpiece and do not apply glue so heavily that it creates "squeeze out" problems. Should there be any glue squeeze out, remove it immediately with a damp rag or paper towel. (See Fig. 3-33.)

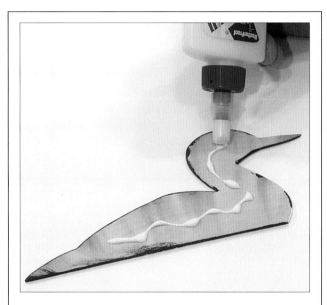

Fig. 3-33: Apply enough glue to do the job, but not so much that will create "squeeze out" problems or excessively thick glue lines.

When all parts are glued in place, remove all dust particles and visually inspect for any problems that may need correcting or touch-up. Using an aerosol, spray the first coat of vinyl or polyurethane finish over the entire project. Sand lightly again, reaching all accessible areas. Attach the wire hanger to the back. Remove sanding dust and apply a final coat of finish.

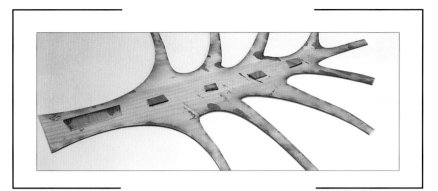

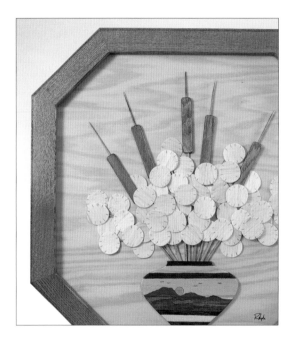

PROJECT NO. 1
CATTAILS

Fig. 4.1-1: An easy project that features techniques used in other projects.

Project No. 1, Cattails, as shown in Fig. 4.1-1 on page 40, requires a vertically rectangular frame as specified in Frame Styles, Fig. 1-3 on page 11. The white painted background is one piece of ⅛"- or ¼"-thick plywood, 18¼" x 30⅛" with horizontal grain. Apply a wash solution of white acrylic paint as discussed in Painting One-piece Backgrounds on page 27. Review Assembly Drawing, Fig. 4.1-2, to familiarize yourself with the layers.

Stack-cut three sets of the Cattail Heads, and cut one set of Reeds and three Stems, using Cattail Patterns, Fig. 4.1-3 on page 42. Stack-cut two sets of the Grasses, using Cattail Pattern, Fig. 4.1-4 on page 43, from two pieces of ⅛"-thick plywood approximately 9½" x 16½". Stain the various pieces.

Assemble the cattails as discussed in Creating Cattails on pages 33–34, and glue them to the backer as shown in Layer 1 below. The stems, reeds and grasses pieces can be cut off at their bottoms to achieve the desired height. The precise placement and sizing of these parts is up to the crafter.

Tip: Wooden skewers can be used for stems and pointed ends. This may require sawing a slot into the upper end of cattail head's bottom layer.

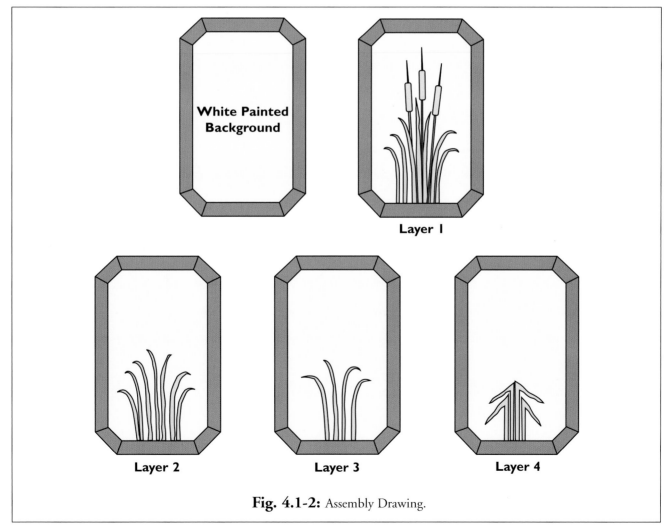

Fig. 4.1-2: Assembly Drawing.

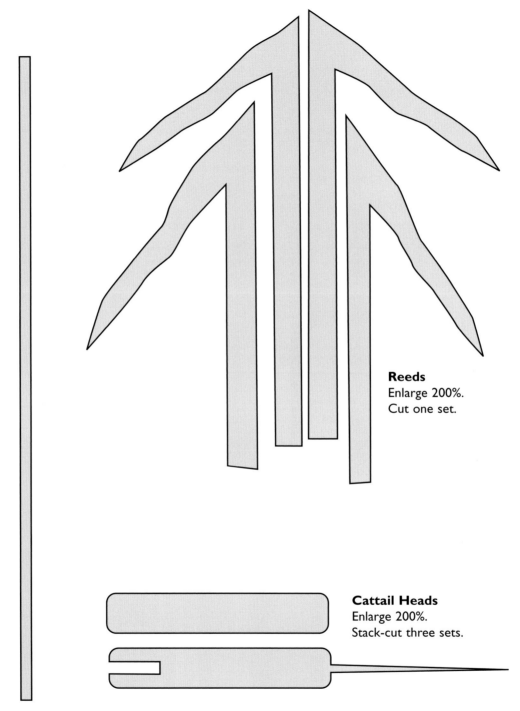

Reeds
Enlarge 200%.
Cut one set.

Cattail Heads
Enlarge 200%.
Stack-cut three sets.

Cattail Stems
⅛" thick, ¼" wide.
Make three. Cut lengths
of 18", 16", and 14½".

Fig. 4.1-3: Cattail Patterns.

Grasses
Stack-cut two sets,
then cut to length
as desired.

Enlarge pattern 200%.

Fig. 4.1-4: Cattail Pattern.

Project No. 2
Silver Dollar Arrangement

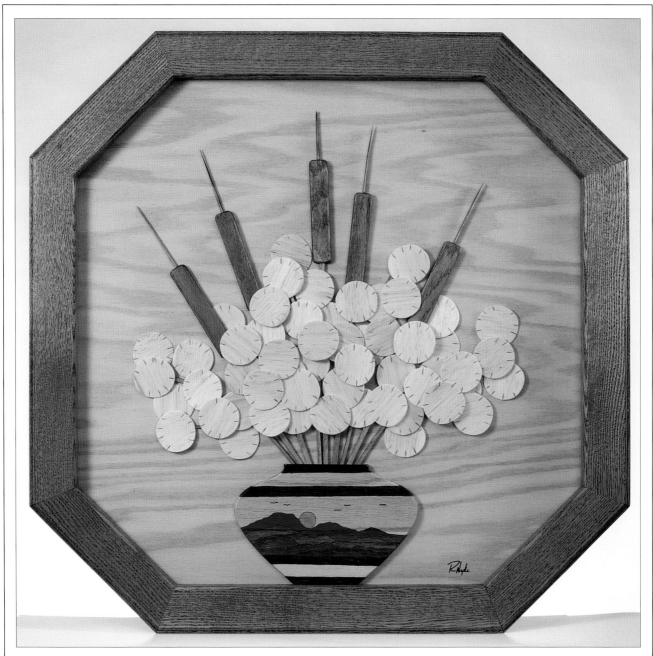

Fig. 4.2-1: Silver Dollar Arrangement combined with cattails.

Project No. 2, Silver Dollar Arrangement, Fig. 4.2-1 on page 44, involves making the same one-piece style of painted background and cattails as those in Project No. 1, Cattails, on page 40. Featured in this project, however, is the addition of silver dollar pieces cut from ⅟₃₂"- or ⅟₁₆"-thick balsa wood which is available from craft and hobby stores. Review Assembly Drawing, Fig. 4.2-2, to familiarize yourself with the layers.

Stack-cut outside profiles of the vase from two pieces of ⅛"-thick birch or oak plywood with horizontal grain. (See Fig. 4.2-3.)

White Painted Background with Horizontal Grain

Layer I

Layer 2

Layer 3

Fig. 4.2-2: Assembly Drawing.

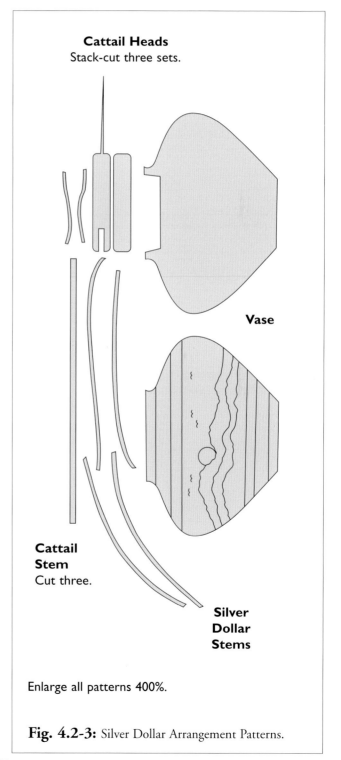

Cattail Heads
Stack-cut three sets.

Vase

Cattail Stem
Cut three.

Silver Dollar Stems

Enlarge all patterns 400%.

Fig. 4.2-3: Silver Dollar Arrangement Patterns.

Separate to complete the sawing of the neck opening in the bottom vase piece. Glue the layers together. Round over the edges and wood-burn the horizontal straight and irregular lines, continuing over the rounded edges. (Refer to Wood-burning Details and Coloring Lines, Fig. 3-9 on page 32.) Stack-cut 8–10 Silver Dollar Pieces at a time, using the patterns in Silver Dollar Arrangement Patterns, Fig. 4.2-4.

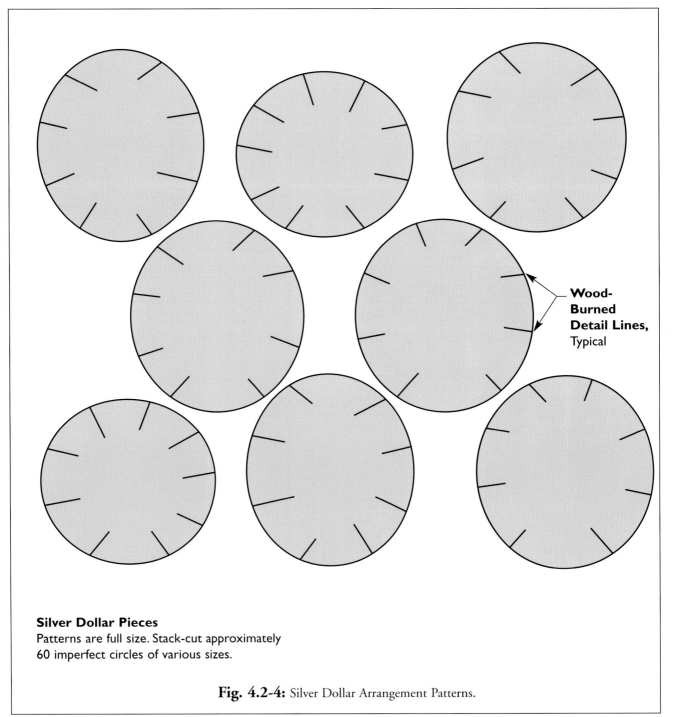

Wood-Burned Detail Lines, Typical

Silver Dollar Pieces
Patterns are full size. Stack-cut approximately 60 imperfect circles of various sizes.

Fig. 4.2-4: Silver Dollar Arrangement Patterns.

Lightly wood-burn the seedpod definition around the inside edge of each silver dollar piece.

Stain and color the vase. Use markers to give it colors similar to those shown in Fig. 4.2-5.

Fig. 4.2-5: Vase section showing wood-burning, natural wood, and stained areas in various shades of brown with the yellow-gold sun.

Glue-assemble all pieces in layers as indicated. (Refer to the Assembly Drawing, Fig. 4.2-2 on page 45.)

Place the silver dollars so there are some open spaces and some of the stem pieces are somewhat visible. (See Fig. 4.2-6.)

Fig. 4.2-6: Close-up of final assembly.

ON THE WING SOUTH

Fig. 4.3-1: This square-framed project features a segmented background, two cut-out geese with fairly detailed wood-burned surfaces, and more cattails and grasses.

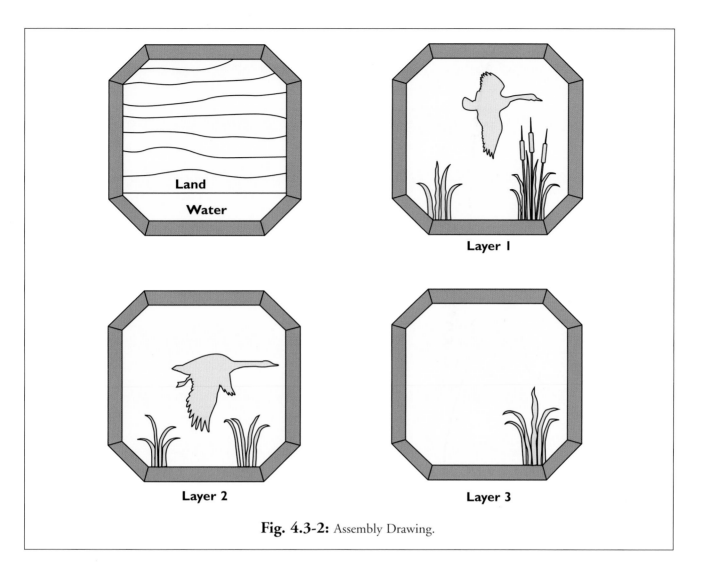

Fig. 4.3-2: Assembly Drawing.

Project No. 3, On the Wing South, Fig. 4.3-1 on page 48, features a square frame and a horizontally segmented background painted white with slightly graduated blue tints toward the top. (Refer to Frame Styles, Fig. 1-3, on page 11, and the Segmented Square Background Pattern, Fig. 2-5 on page 17.) Again, we find cattails and grasses, made as discussed in Project Nos. 1 and 2.

Review Assembly Drawing, Fig. 4.3-2, to familiarize yourself with the layers. Review the techniques in Making Segmented Backgrounds on pages 22–23. Notice how this background consists of blue water at the bottom under irregular green land and white to light blue sky pieces. A graduated white-blue sky can be achieved by gradually adding some blue acrylic to the whitewash, increasing the percentage of blue for each successive piece.

When dry, glue the segments to a backer and attach the cured assembly to the back of the frame. (Refer to Fastening the Background to the Frame on page 28.)

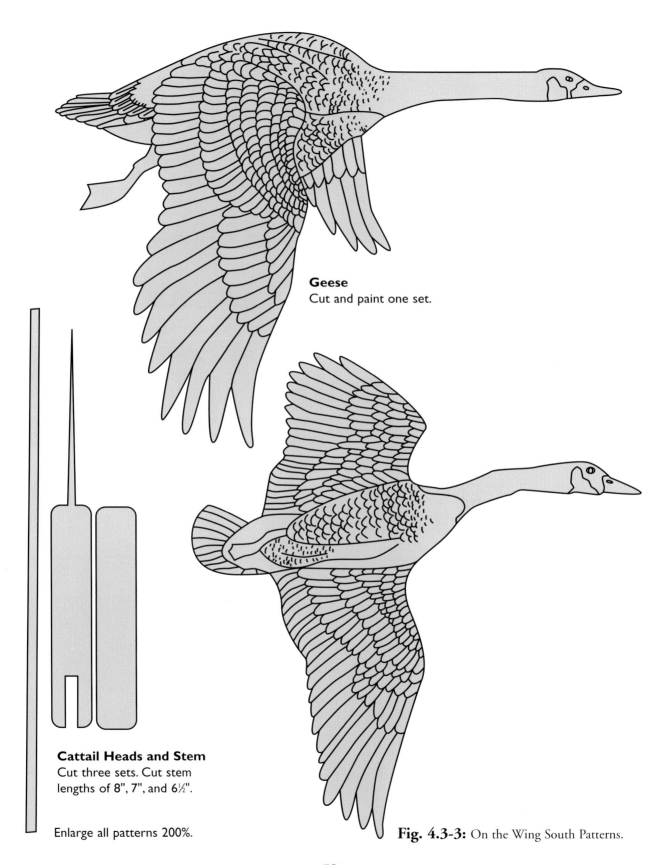

Geese
Cut and paint one set.

Cattail Heads and Stem
Cut three sets. Cut stem
lengths of 8", 7", and 6½".

Enlarge all patterns 200%.

Fig. 4.3-3: On the Wing South Patterns.

Cut out the Geese and Cattail Heads and Stems, using On the Wing South Patterns, Fig. 4.3-3 on page 50. Transfer all lines to ⅛"-thick plywood. (Refer to Patterns, Layout, and Cutting Layers on pages 30–32.) Round over the edges and wood-burn the detail and definition lines. The burning must be well done so visual texture shows through the brown and white coloring. Notice how the wing tips, shoulders, and neck graduate to deep browns, colored with markers. White areas are painted with full-strength white acrylic paint. (See Fig. 4.3-4.)

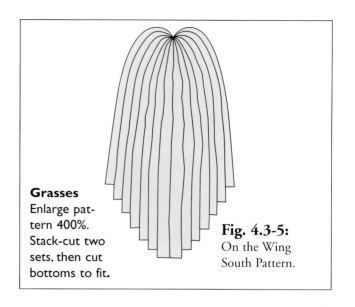

Grasses
Enlarge pattern 400%. Stack-cut two sets, then cut bottoms to fit.

Fig. 4.3-5: On the Wing South Pattern.

Fig. 4.3-4: Close-up of typical painting details.

Cut the Grasses, using the On the Wing South Pattern, Fig. 4.3-5. Finish as shown in Fig. 4.3-6.

Fig. 4.3-6: Cattails and grasses. The bottoms of all grasses must be cut off for lengths and fitting.

Gluing down the various parts is pretty straightforward. The wing of the larger goose in Layer 2 is placed over a ⅛"-thick shim.

51

PROJECT NO. 4
APPLE TREE

Fig. 4.4-1: The Apple Tree project involves many easy-to-make pieces. The guided assembly illustrations simplify this process as well.

Project No. 4, Apple Tree, Fig. 4.4-1 on page 52, has more parts than most projects, and its assembly is somewhat complicated. The parts, however, are all easy to make and finish. The Assembly Drawing, Fig. 4.4-2, and the accompanying photos will be helpful during the assembly process.

Overall, this project is not difficult; it is labor-intensive but well worth the effort. You may elect to color the apples as you wish. The color brown was selected to create a little visual excitement. An interesting option is to make the tree without the apples.

The project requires a round frame and a one-piece plywood backer, ⅛" or ¼" thick, with horizontal grain and a 50:50 acrylic-whitewashed surface. (See Fig. 4.4-3, and refer to to Frame Styles, Fig. 1-4 on page 12 and Painting One-piece Backgrounds on page 27.)

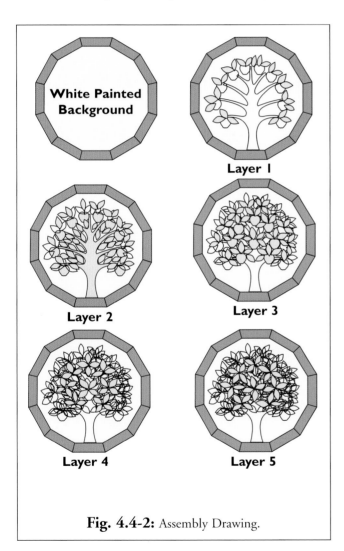

Fig. 4.4-2: Assembly Drawing.

Fig. 4.4-3: One-piece painted background has acrylic wash of white.

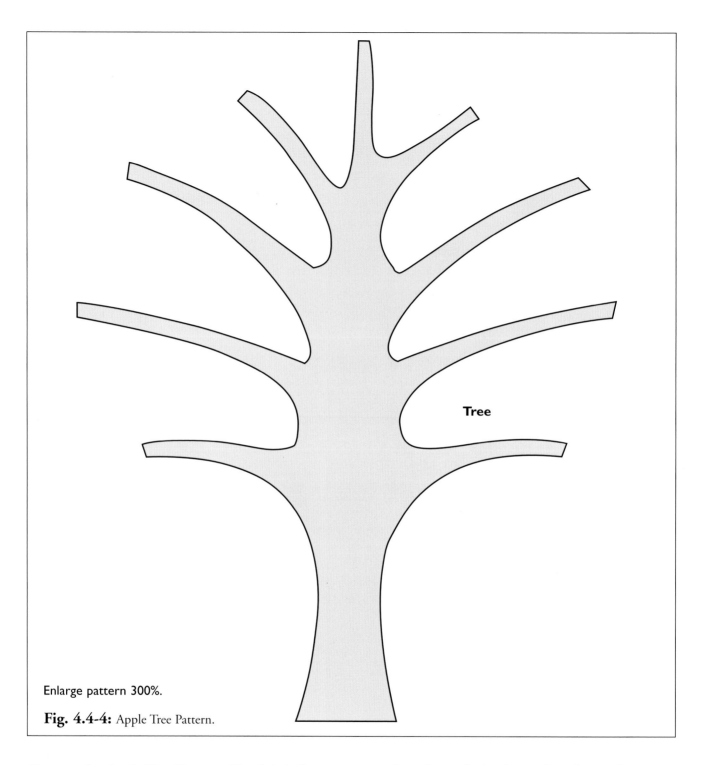

Tree

Enlarge pattern 300%.

Fig. 4.4-4: Apple Tree Pattern.

Cut out the Apple Tree Pattern, Fig. 4.4-4, from ⅛"-thick plywood. The project requires 18 apples, all ¼" thick with vertical grain and rounded edges. Use ¼"-thick plywood or make them from two layers of ⅛"-thick plywood approxi-mately 10" x 12" glued together, face to face. Approximately 200–225 leaves of different sizes cut from ⅛"-thick straight-grain plywood are required. (See Apple Tree Patterns, Fig. 4.4-5, on page 55.)

Apples
Pattern is full size. Make ¼" thick. Stack-cut 18.

Leaves
Patterns are full size. Make ⅛" thick. Stack-cut 20–21.

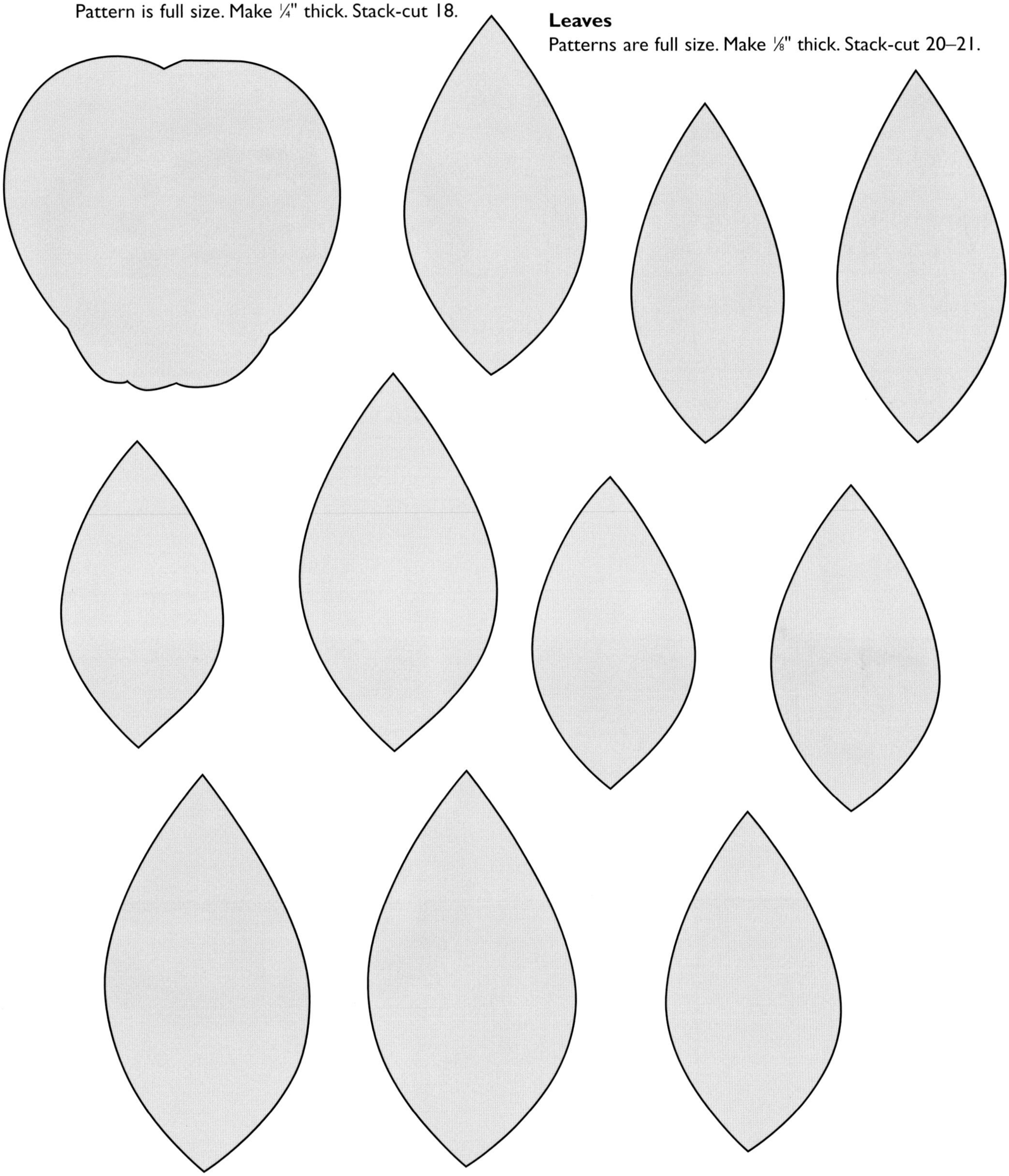

Fig. 4.4-5: Apple Tree Patterns.

Tip: To save time, stack-cut as many layers of apples and leaves as your scroll saw will cut easily. The grain of the leaves should always run point to point. To save time, after slightly rounding and sanding the edges, dip the apples and leaves into two pans containing walnut and light oak stains respectively.

Assembly. After attaching the painted background to the rear of the frame, prepare the tree for assembly by gluing several ⅛"-thick shims to the back side. (See Fig. 4.4-6.)

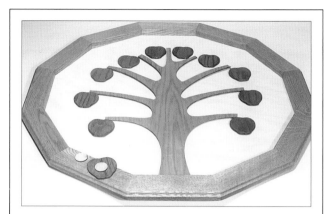

Fig. 4.4-7: Layer 1 in ¼" relief. Also shown on the frame are ⅛"-thick shims.

Next, add more leaves, 2–3 for each apple, with the leaf point pointing toward an imaginary apple stem. Use shims under the leaves of Layer 2, filling in spaces between the branches. Do not cover any apple entirely. (See Fig. 4.4-8, below, and refer to Assembly Drawing, Fig. 4.4-2 on page 53.)

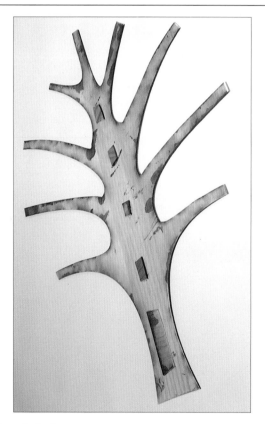

Fig. 4.4-6: Tree, finished and prepared with ⅛"-thick shims glued to its back, ready to be glued down.

Fig. 4.4-8: Leaves glued directly to the backer.

Glue the tree down. Next, place 10 apples with ⅛"-thick shims under each. The purpose of this is to allow some leaves to slide under portions of the apples. (See Fig. 4.4-7.)

Now, glue down the last eight apples of Layer 3, along with more leaves. (See Fig. 4.4-9, below, and refer to Assembly Drawing, Fig. 4.4-2 on page 53.)

Fig. 4.4-9: Layer 3 with remaining apples.

The leaves should be arranged in groups of 3–4 with their points together, pointing toward the stem of the apple. Remember to use small shims wherever necessary to provide an inconspicuous and elevated gluing surface. Since the apples are ¼" thick, add more leaves to complete a level equal to the top surface of the apples. (See Figs. 4.4-10 through 4.4-12.)

Fig. 4.4-10: Assembly about 80% complete.

Fig. 4.4-11: Layers 4 and 5. Apples have more of their surfaces covered than actually exposed.

Fig. 4.4-12: Leaves applied in groups of three or four. More layers of leaves are applied to the central area of the tree.

PROJECT NO. 5
CALIFORNIA COAST

Fig. 4.5-1: The California Coast project features colorful sailboats with layered landforms and trees.

Project No. 5, California Coast, Fig. 4.5-1 on page 58, is easy to make. It requires an oval frame and a one-piece painted background made from ⅛"- or ¼"-thick plywood with horizontal grain. (Refer to Frame Styles, Fig. 1-4 on page 12.) The layered pieces are all cut from ⅛"-thick plywood. Review Assembly Drawing, Fig. 4.5-2, to familiarize yourself with the layers.

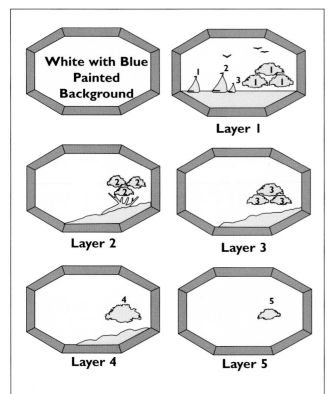

Fig. 4.5-2: Assembly Drawing. Notice in Layer 2 that the edge of the tree and landform patterns have the same irregular cuts.

The background is a painted white acrylic wash with blue streaking. (Refer to Painting White with Blue Streaks on page 27.) Attach the painted background to the frame. (Refer to Fastening the Background to the Frame on page 28.)

Cut the Water and Landform pieces, using the California Coast Patterns in Fig. 4.5-3. The water should be cut from horizontal grain.

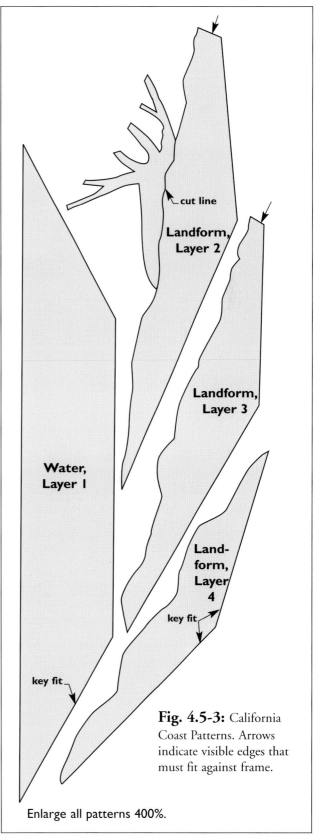

Fig. 4.5-3: California Coast Patterns. Arrows indicate visible edges that must fit against frame.

Enlarge all patterns 400%.

Select rotary-cut open or wide grain to simulate waves of water. (See 4.5-4, below, and refer to Fig. 4.5-1 on page 58.)

Fig. 4.5-4: Notice the grain of the piece selected for the water.

The grain of the landforms can run somewhat obliquely, depending upon the plywood patterns available. Notice in Fig. 4.5-6, and the Assembly Drawing, Fig. 4.5-2, Layer 2, on page 59, that the lower edge of the cypress tree matches the upper edge of the landform. This is cut simultaneously from the same piece to achieve a perfect fit. Also notice that the left edge of the water and the right edge of the smallest landform piece must be fitted to the edges of the frame as indicated by the "key fit" notes and arrows on the patterns. (Refer to California Coast Patterns, Fig. 4.5-3, on page 59.)

It is best to cut all of the Treetop Layers from the same or similar-figured wood for uniformity, using the California Coast Patterns, Fig. 4.5-5.)

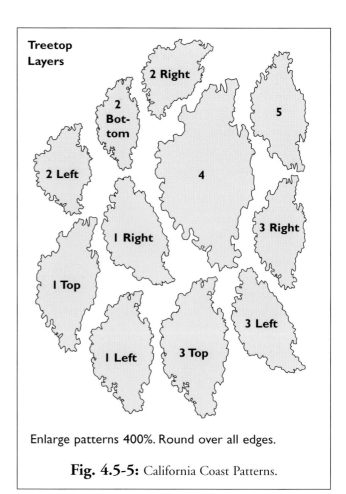

Treetop Layers

Enlarge patterns 400%. Round over all edges.

Fig. 4.5-5: California Coast Patterns.

Fig. 4.5-6: Close-up of the tree and landforms.

Use a small rotary tool and burr, a flap sander, or a round file to roughly round over the edges of the various tree pieces.

Cut out the Boats and Gulls, using the California Coast Patterns, Fig. 4.5-7. Wood-burn the detail lines of the sailboats. Stain and color all pieces. (Refer to Fig. 4.5-4 on page 60 as a guide.) Use acrylic paint for the boat hulls and colored markers for the sails. Glue down all pieces.

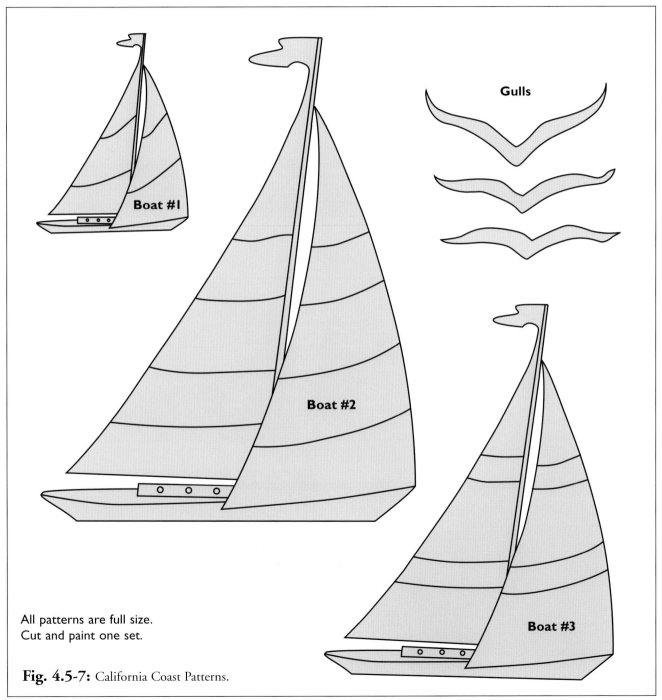

Gulls

Boat #1

Boat #2

Boat #3

All patterns are full size.
Cut and paint one set.

Fig. 4.5-7: California Coast Patterns.

CHAPTER 5
INTERMEDIATE PROJECTS

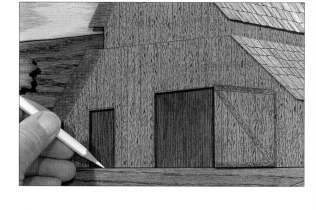

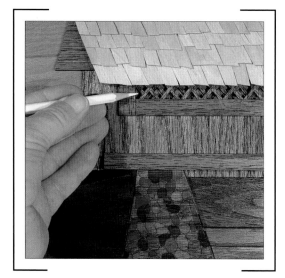

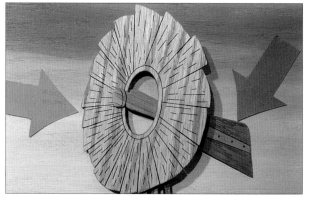

MONTEREY SUNSET

Fig. 5.6-1: This project incorporates the same layered tree as the California Coast project, and features a segmented background of concentric circles with graduated coloring shown here in red-orange tones.

Project No. 6, Monterey Sunset, Fig. 5.6-1 on page 63, is much like the California Coast project, with the same tree patterns and the same style of landforms. Review Assembly Drawing, Fig. 5.6-2, to familiarize yourself with the layers.

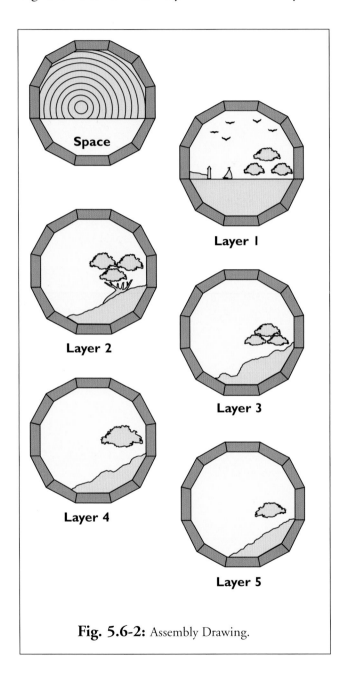

Fig. 5.6-2: Assembly Drawing.

The visual emphasis of this project, however, is the dramatic segmented background within a round frame. (See Fig. 5.6-3.)

Fig. 5.6-3: Blue sky tones are an alternate background choice.

This project requires a segmented round background cut from a piece of ⅛" or ¼" x 17½" x 26" plywood. (Refer to Segmented Backgrounds, Fig. 2-7 on page 19.) Cut the background from ⅛"- or ¼"-thick plywood with horizontal grain. This project will also require a backer of thin plywood 26" square.

Layout the Background. Trace the inside of the frame lightly with a pencil and add 1" all around. Locate the center point of the sun and the circles by measuring from the edges of the background. (See Fig. 5.6-4 on page 65, and refer to Segmented Backgrounds, Fig. 2-9 on page 21, for complete layout details.)

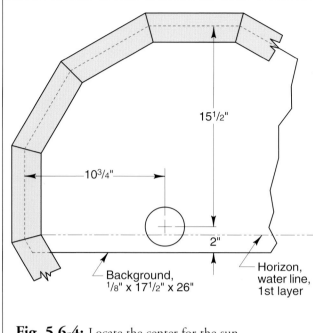

Fig. 5.6-4: Locate the center for the sun.

Use a strip of thin wood, with pencil holes spaced 1½" apart, to lay out the segmented circles. (See Fig. 5.6-5.)

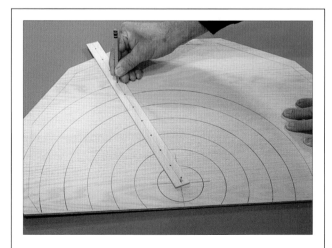

Fig. 5.6-5: Layout circular segments.

Carefully saw each ring. Refer to Sawing Segmented Backgrounds, Fig. 2-16 on page 24. Round over all mating edges with a ¹⁄₁₆" radius. (See Fig. 5.6-6.)

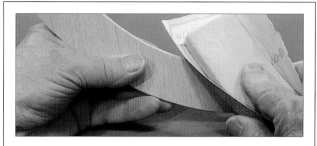

Fig. 5.6-6: Rounding over segment edges with coarse abrasive.

Color the Sky Pieces. Begin with a yellow-gold mixture of water and acrylic paint for a red-orange sky. (Use a white-and-blue mixture for a background with a blue sky). Mix two teaspoons of bright yellow paint into one cup of water for for the first ring around the sun. (See Figs. 5.6-7 through 5.6-10, below and on page 66.)

Fig. 5.6-7: Preparing to paint the graduated yellow to red-orange segments.

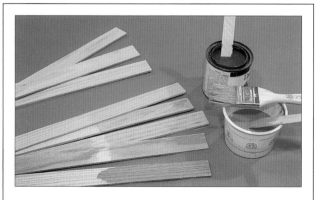

Fig. 5.6-8: Scraps for testing color mixture ratios.

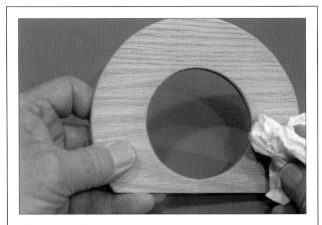

Fig. 5.6-9: Wiping with a paper towel.

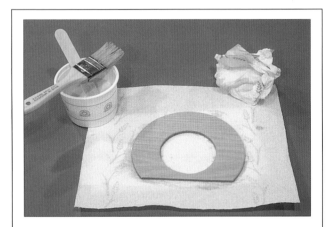

Fig. 5.6-10: First piece completed.

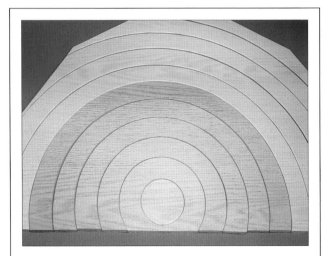

Fig. 5.6-11: Background partly colored.

Apply the diluted colors on test pieces and wipe. Adjust color mixture ratios if necessary. After color is established for the first ring, begin to add red pigment beginning with ⅛ of a teaspoon. Add more pigment, increasing the ratio for each successive piece until the last piece is painted. The final piece should be a vivid red-orange color. (Refer to Fig. 5.6-11.)

Glue the segmented pieces to a full plywood backer. (See Fig. 5.6-12, below.)

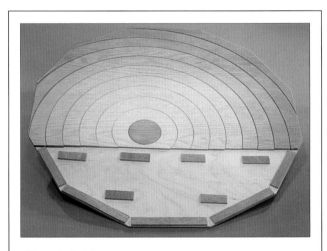

Fig. 5.6-12: Completed background glued to a backer along with some ⅛"-thick spacers.

Make and finish all of the layer pieces. (See the Monterey Sunset Patterns, Figs. 5.6-13, 5.6-14, and 5.6-15 on pages 67–68.)

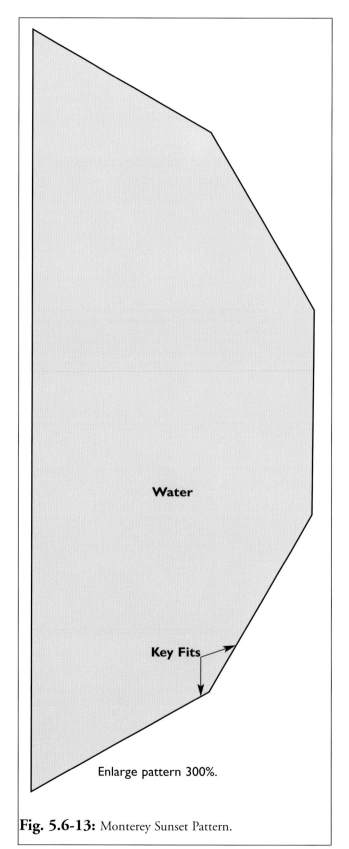

Water

Key Fits

Enlarge pattern 300%.

Fig. 5.6-13: Monterey Sunset Pattern.

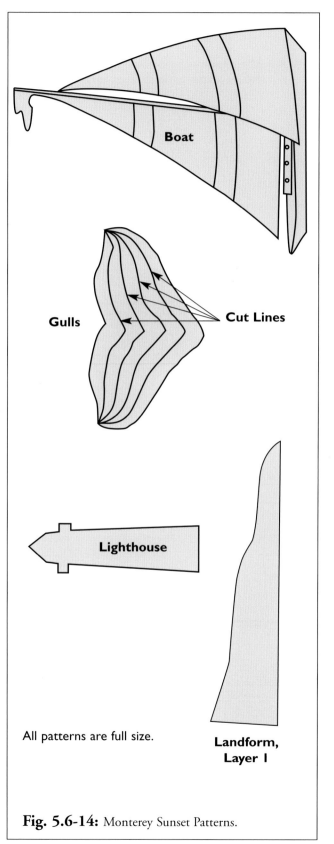

Boat

Gulls

Cut Lines

Lighthouse

All patterns are full size.

Landform, Layer 1

Fig. 5.6-14: Monterey Sunset Patterns.

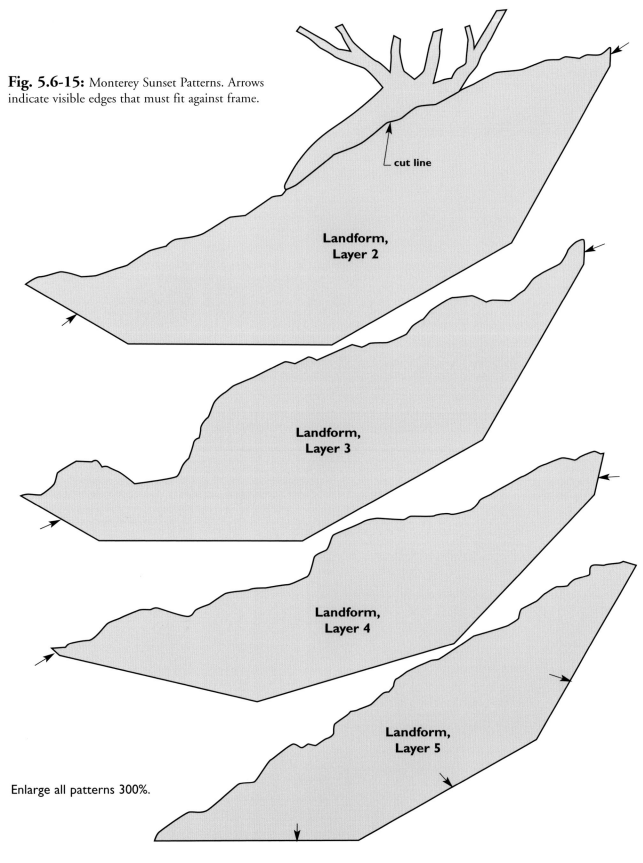

Fig. 5.6-15: Monterey Sunset Patterns. Arrows indicate visible edges that must fit against frame.

cut line

Landform, Layer 2

Landform, Layer 3

Landform, Layer 4

Landform, Layer 5

Enlarge all patterns 300%.

Lightly trace the cutting lines for water piece, following the inside frame edge.

Fig. 5.6-16: Lightly trace cutting lines.

The water and landform layers are similar to the ones used in the California Coast project, Fig. 4.5-3, on page 59. Before attaching the background (with the backer) to the frame, cut and make the key fits on the left edge of the water piece and the right edges of the fifth layer of the hillside.

The tree top patterns are exactly the same as those used in Project No. 5, California Coast, and are found in Fig. 4.5-5 on page 60.

Tip: When finishing the landforms, use four different shades of brown acrylic or oil stains and randomly blend in a little green. The tree-tops are stained a dark brown and the trunk a light brown.

(See Figs. 5.6-17 and 5.6-18, and refer to Monterey Sunset Patterns, Fig. 5.6-14 on page 67 and Fig. 5.6-15 on page 68.) .

Fig. 5.6-17: The water overlaps the sky and the sailboat covers the "compass" nail hole made in the center of the sun and butts against the top edge of the water.

Fig. 5.6-18: Completed tree and layered landforms. Notice the edges of the last landform layer that fits perfectly to the inside edge of the frame.

It is a good idea to leave the gluing of the gulls for last so they can be more artistically placed.

Position the Tree Pieces. First, place all pieces without glue on the background. Then remove all but the Layer 1 pieces and glue them down in their established locations. Glue down the remaining treetop layers and the landform pieces. Assure that the edges of those pieces that will be visible fit tightly against the inside edges of the frame.

PROJECT NO. 7
THE GATHERING

Fig. 5.7-1: The specific features of this project are the segmented background simulating twilight and the realistic coloring of the deer.

The key to Project No. 7, The Gathering, Fig. 5.7-1, is coloring the deer realistically.

Make the rectangular frame. (Refer to Frame Styles, Fig. 1-3 on page 11, and Segmented Backgrounds, Fig. 2-6 on page 18.)

Review Assembly Drawing, Fig. 5.7-2 on page 71, to familiarize yourself with the layers. Cut the moon from the same piece as the background and align the grain for continuity. Finish the background to simulate dusk. Paint the moon bright white. Color the bottom landform piece a deep brown. Color the bottom skyline piece with a wash of 25:75 white acrylic and water with some blue added for the first piece. Then add proportionally more blue pigment with each successive piece with the darkest coloring at the top.

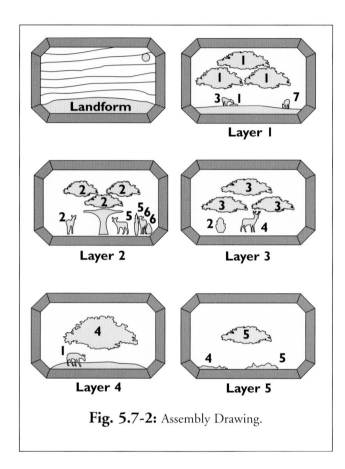

Fig. 5.7-2: Assembly Drawing.

Cut out the tree pieces, using The Gathering Patterns, Fig. 5.7-3 at right and Fig. 5.7-4 on page 72. Notice that patterns in 5.7-3 are enlarged 400% and those in 5.7-4 on page 72 are enlarged 300%. Round over all edges. Color the treetops deep brown.

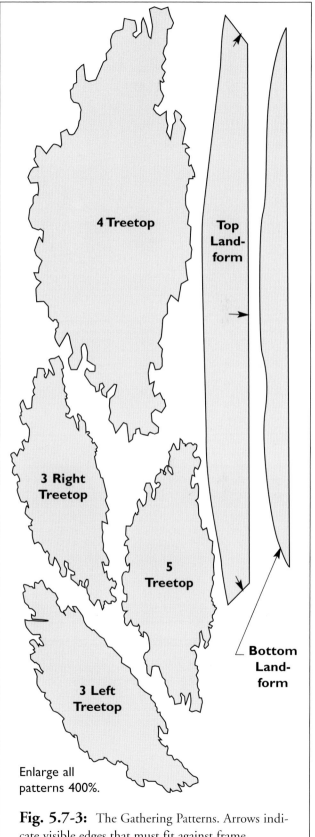

Enlarge all patterns 400%.

Fig. 5.7-3: The Gathering Patterns. Arrows indicate visible edges that must fit against frame.

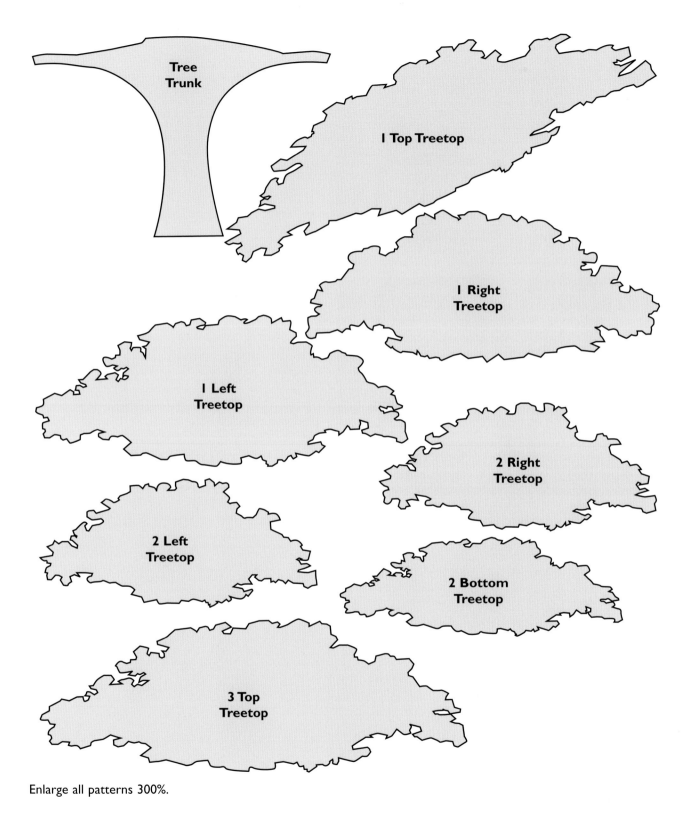

Enlarge all patterns 300%.

Fig. 5.7-4: The Gathering Patterns.

Cut Figs. 5.7-5, below, and 5.7-6 on page 74. Color the bushes a dark green. Plan to cut out a few extra deer or use some scraps on which to practice painting. It will be well worth the time and effort because the deer in other projects require the same techniques. The correct coloring and the wood-burned detailing of the deer are very important. Review the instructions and figures given in Making and Coloring Deer on pages 36–37. It is suggested that a few practice deerhead cutouts be made and painted before undertaking the seven required for this project. When confident the coloring is correct, paint each step on all seven at once as appropriate.

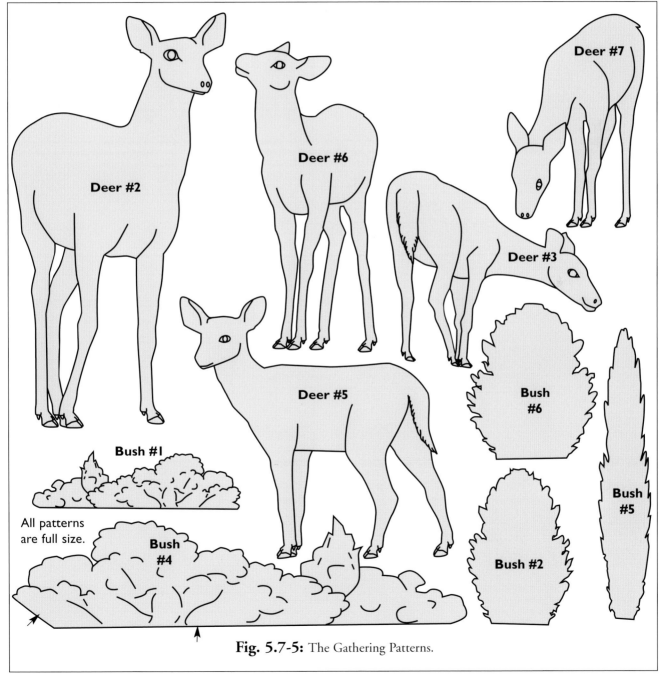

Fig. 5.7-5: The Gathering Patterns.

Deer #1

Deer #4

Bush #5

All patterns are full size.

Fig. 5.7-6: The Gathering Patterns.

Tips: Study Fig. 5.7-7. Place ⅛"-thick shims under the tree trunk to support the other tree pieces as necessary. Also place small shims under the Deer #1, #2, #5, and #6.

Fig. 5.7-7: Close-up showing landforms and placement of four deer.

PROJECT NO. 8
LAKE REGATTA

Fig. 5.8-1: Vivid transparent colors highlight this nautical scene.

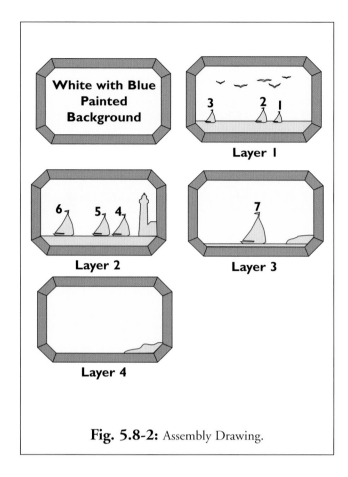

White with Blue Painted Background

Layer 1

Layer 2

Layer 3

Layer 4

Fig. 5.8-2: Assembly Drawing.

Project No. 8, Lake Regatta, Fig. 5.8-1 on page 76, features bright colors and some detailed wood-burning. The experienced scroller may elect to use a 2/0 blade and cut out some of the fine, detailed spacings at the top of the lighthouse or simply burn-in all details.

(Refer to Frame Styles, Fig. 1-3 on page 11 and Painting One-piece Backgrounds on page 27.)

Review Assembly Drawing, Fig. 5.8-2, to familiarize yourself with the layers.

Cut out and wood-burn the detail on all of the parts according to the patterns. (See Fig. 5.8-3 at right and Figs. 5.8-4 through 5.8-6 on pages 78–80.)

Boat #1

Boat #2

Boat #4

Boat #3

Lighthouse

Enlarge all patterns 200%.

Fig. 5.8-3: Lake Regattta Patterns.

77

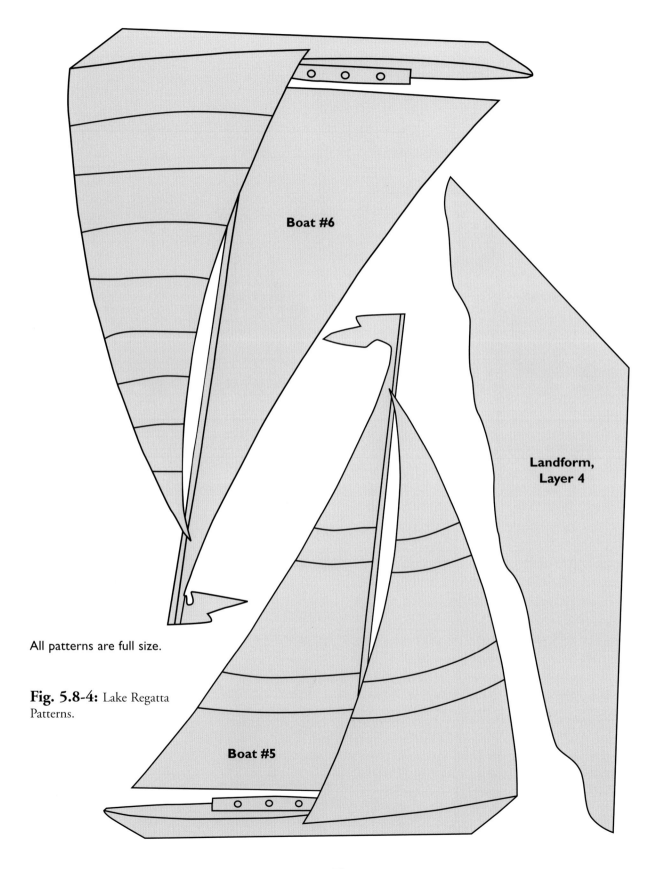

Boat #6

Landform, Layer 4

All patterns are full size.

Fig. 5.8-4: Lake Regatta Patterns.

Boat #5

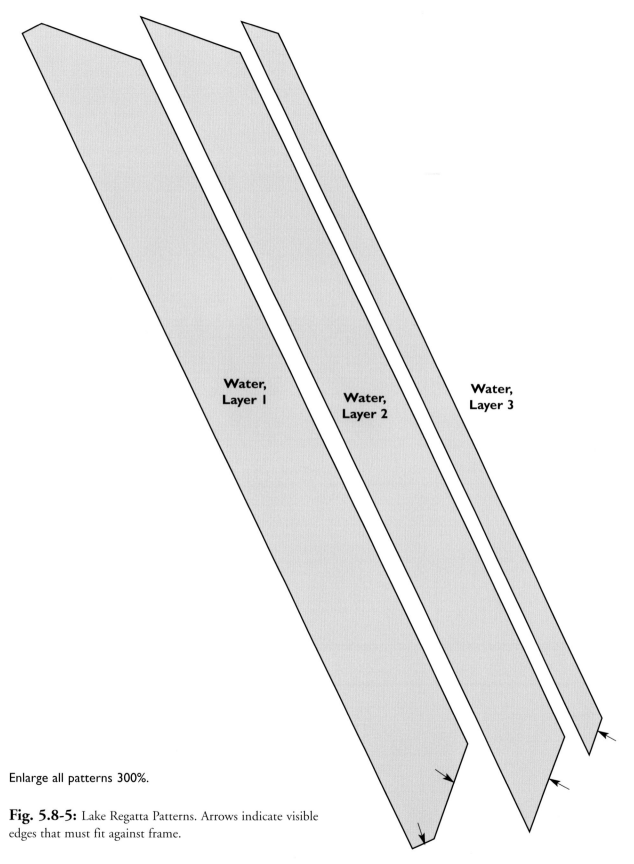

Water, Layer 1

Water, Layer 2

Water, Layer 3

Enlarge all patterns 300%.

Fig. 5.8-5: Lake Regatta Patterns. Arrows indicate visible edges that must fit against frame.

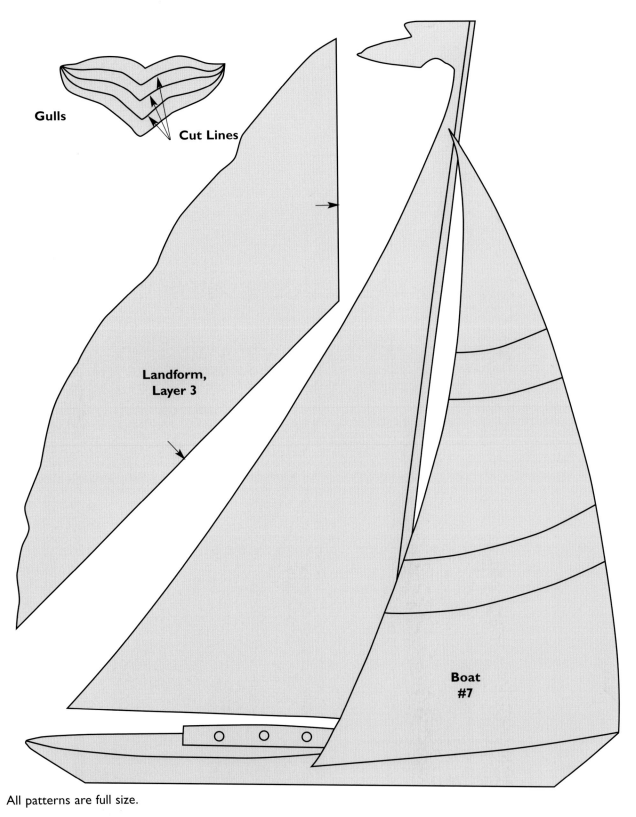

Gulls

Cut Lines

Landform, Layer 3

Boat #7

All patterns are full size.

Fig. 5.8-6: Lake Regatta Patterns. Arrows indicate visible edges that must fit against frame.

Cut all three water pieces from the same piece of wood so they have the same color intensity when painted. Use horizontal grain for the sailboats. Remember that good wood-burned detail lines are necessary to prevent the marker coloring from bleeding across the line. The boat hulls are painted with undiluted acrylic paint. (Refer to Wood-burning Details and Coloring Lines, Figs. 3-9 through 3-11, on page 32, and Finishing with Felt-tip Markers, Figs. 3-12 through 3-13 on pages 32–33.)

Use a brownish or gray acrylic wash for coloring the two shoreline pieces and a dark blue for the water pieces. The lighthouse is diluted white acrylic paint and all else is colored with markers.

Glue down the parts following the sequence given on the Assembly Drawing, Fig. 5.8-2 on page 77. Place well-hidden shims under the four larger sailboats.

See Figs. 5.8-7 and 5.8-8 for some additional assembly hints.

Fig. 5.8-7: Close-up showing finely-cut detail at top of lighthouse.

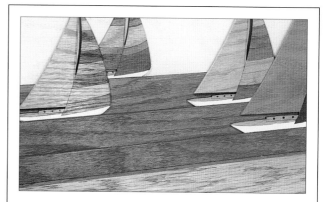

Fig. 5.8-8: Notice how the sailboats sit on the top edge of the three water pieces.

PROJECT NO. 9
BALLOON RACE

Fig. 5.9-1: This is truly a fun project to make because the eye-catching coloring is so easy to achieve with markers and the assembly is not complicated. Notice the open grain used on the land area.

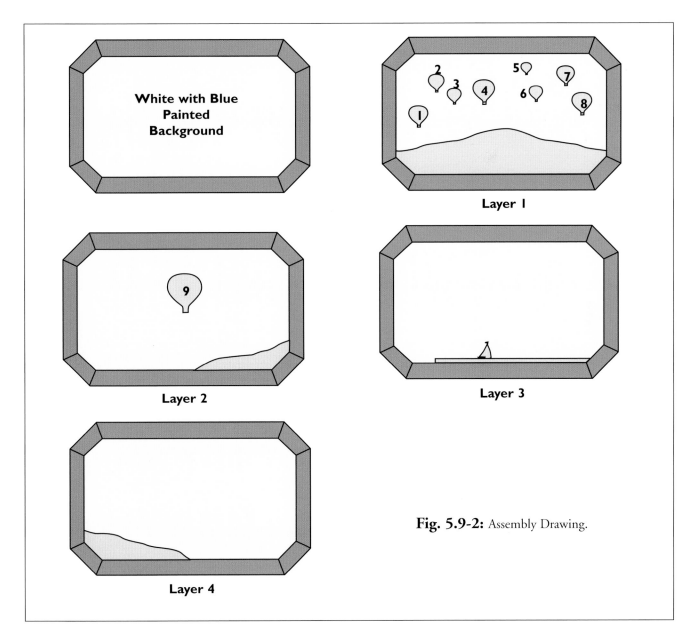

White with Blue Painted Background

Layer 1

Layer 2

Layer 3

Fig. 5.9-2: Assembly Drawing.

Layer 4

All of the bright colors of Project No. 9, Balloon Race, Fig. 5.9-1 on page 82 came from school-type markers. The project is built with the rectangular frame and a one-piece painted backer. (Refer to Frame Styles, Fig. 1-3 on page 11 and Painting One-piece Backgrounds on page 27.)

Review Assembly Drawing, Fig. 5.9-2, to familiarize yourself with the layers. The nine balloon and sailboat patterns are given at half size. Notice that each pattern has the balloon's basket pattern

connected to the bottom, which must be cut free. Use ⅛"-thick plywood with vertical grain. Round the edges and burn in the color-separating detail lines continuing over the rounded edges. Assure that the wood-burned detail lines are deep enough to prevent the marker colors from bleeding across the line. (See Fig. 5.9-3 on page 84 and refer to Wood-burning Details and Coloring Lines, Figs. 3-9 through 3-11, on page 32, and Finishing with Felt-tip Markers, Figs. 3-12 through 3-13 on pages 32–33.)

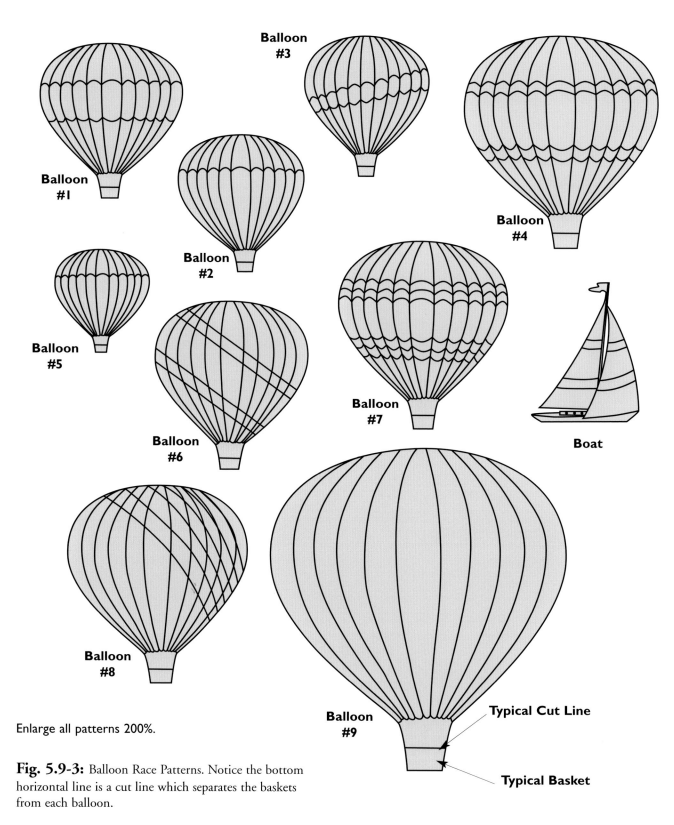

Balloon #3

Balloon #1

Balloon #2

Balloon #4

Balloon #5

Balloon #6

Balloon #7

Boat

Balloon #8

Balloon #9

Typical Cut Line

Typical Basket

Enlarge all patterns 200%.

Fig. 5.9-3: Balloon Race Patterns. Notice the bottom horizontal line is a cut line which separates the baskets from each balloon.

Color the balloons using vividly-colored markers. It may be necessary to coat more than once to achieve higher color intensities. Remember that new markers are "juicier" than used ones and to always apply the lighter colors first. Should there be any bleeding across the burned lines, darker colors are more likely to cover. (See Fig. 5.9-4.)

Use three different shades of deep browns to color the landforms and dark blue to color the water. Finally, glue down the layers.

Tips: The large landform piece of layer one does not need to fit perfectly against the frame because the pieces in layers two and four will cover the ends. The landform piece in layer two must fit well on the right side and layer four must fit well against the frame on the bottom and left side. The large balloon (Balloon #9) must have a ⅛"-thick shim under its right side.

Fig. 5.9-5: The large balloon (#9) overlaps Balloon #4 on the left and requires a ⅛"-thick shim, located under the right half.

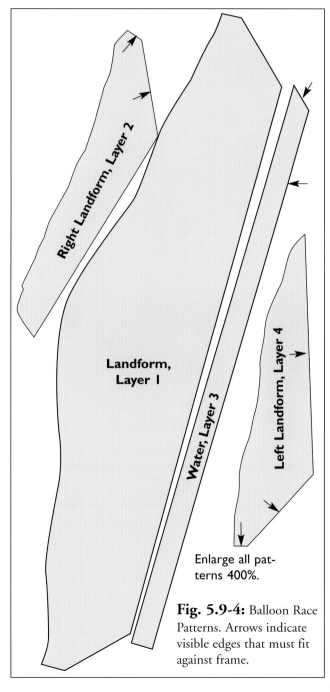

Right Landform, Layer 2

Landform, Layer I

Water, Layer 3

Left Landform, Layer 4

Enlarge all patterns 400%.

Fig. 5.9-4: Balloon Race Patterns. Arrows indicate visible edges that must fit against frame.

PROJECT No. 10
BACK TO THE GARDEN

Fig. 5.10-1: Typical rural barn scene.

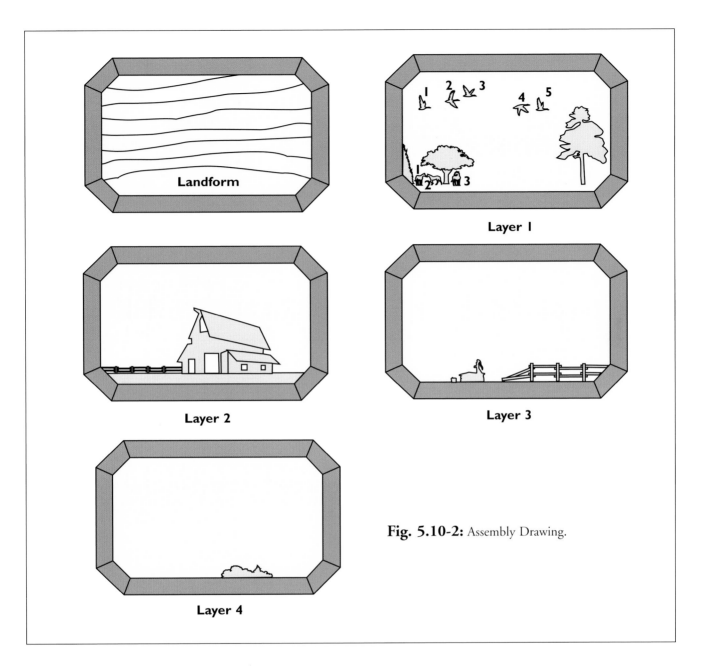

Landform

Layer 1

Layer 2

Layer 3

Fig. 5.10-2: Assembly Drawing.

Layer 4

Project No. 10, Back to the Garden, Fig. 5.10-1 on page 86 involves making a rectangular frame and a segmented background. (Refer to Frame Styles, Fig. 1-3 on page 11, and Segmented Backgrounds, Fig. 2-6 on page 18. The background is painted in shades of blue, and dark green grass with a little brown added to mute the green. Review Assembly Drawing, Fig. 5.10-2, to familiarize yourself with the layers. Use the patterns for all layering pieces given in Figs. 5.10-3 through 5.10-6 on pages 88–91.

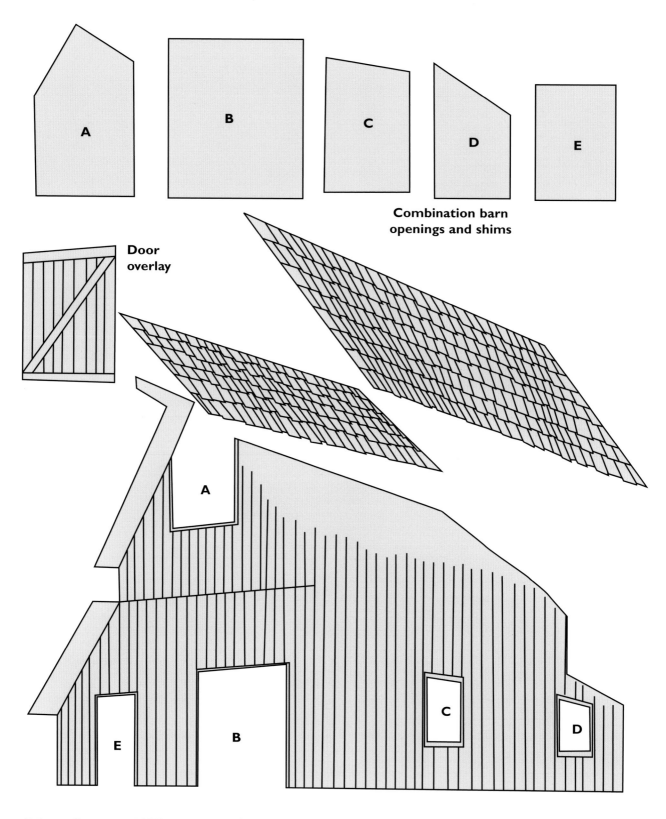

A

B

C

D

E

Combination barn openings and shims

Door overlay

A

E   B

C

D

Enlarge all patterns 200%.

Fig. 5.10-3: Back to the Garden Patterns.

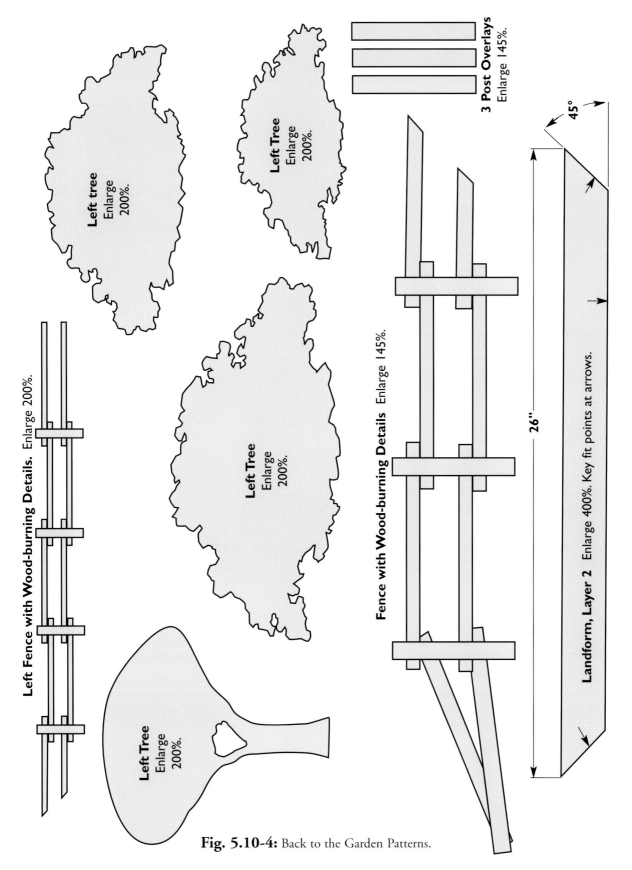

Left tree
Enlarge 200%.

Left Tree
Enlarge 200%.

Left Tree
Enlarge 200%.

Left Tree
Enlarge 200%.

3 Post Overlays
Enlarge 145%.

Left Fence with Wood-burning Details. Enlarge 200%.

Fence with Wood-burning Details Enlarge 145%.

45°

26"

Landform, Layer 2 Enlarge 400%. Key fit points at arrows.

Fig. 5.10-4: Back to the Garden Patterns.

89

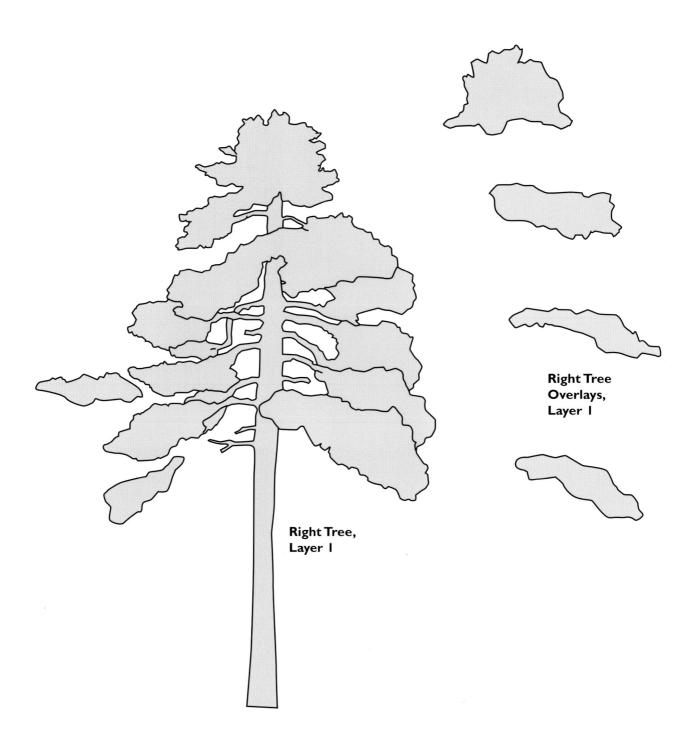

Right Tree Overlays, Layer 1

Right Tree, Layer 1

Enlarge all patterns 200%.

Fig. 5.10-5: Back to the Garden Patterns.

90

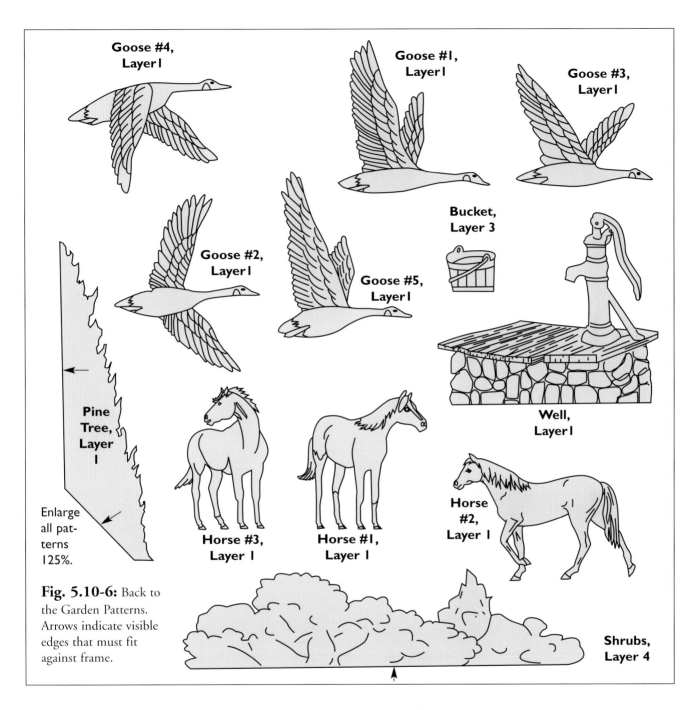

Goose #4, Layer 1

Goose #1, Layer 1

Goose #3, Layer 1

Goose #2, Layer 1

Goose #5, Layer 1

Bucket, Layer 3

Pine Tree, Layer 1

Well, Layer 1

Enlarge all patterns 125%.

Horse #3, Layer 1

Horse #1, Layer 1

Horse #2, Layer 1

Fig. 5.10-6: Back to the Garden Patterns. Arrows indicate visible edges that must fit against frame.

Shrubs, Layer 4

Select tight vertically grained wood for the barn. This will lessen the need for intensive wood-burned details. Select material for the roof that does not have distinct grain patterns or figure that would visually conflict with the shingle texturing. The shingle details are wood-burned and then given a transparent gray coloring with an acrylic wash of gray (white mixed with black).

The red of the barn is a wash of 50:50 red acrylic and water. The underside of the roof along the left of the barn should be colored a darker red to indicate shadows.

The grain of the left tree trunk runs vertically with horizontal grain for the tops. (See Fig. 5.10-7 on page 92.)

Fig. 5.10-7: Trees in Layer 1 with barn temporarily in place. Notice the horizontal grain of the treetop.

The right tree has all horizontal grain with some wood-burning detail and applied overlays. The trunks of the trees are partial shims for the land-form of Layer 2. (Refer to Fig. 5.10-5 on page 90 and see Fig. 5.10-8.)

Fig. 5.10-8: Notice that all parts of this tree have horizontal grain.

The left tree can be any fall color. Notice that the treetops of both trees have darker colored edges. This is achieved by applying a second coat and blending it into the first coat.

Color the fence pieces a weathered gray, and duplicate the coloring of the horses and pump pieces as closely as possible to Fig. 5.10-1 on page 86. Use six or seven marker colors including reds, browns, grays, and tans to color the stone work. Apply a final light gray over the stonework with a marker to blend all of the "stones."

Though the geese are small, they should be colored with care and as realistically as possible. Refer to Painting the Small Geese on pages 34–36 for step-by-step instructions and photos illustrating this important process.

Assemble the barn as one unit. Use the pieces that replicate the dark interiors of the door and window openings as visible shims to raise the barn to the level of the animals and the tree of the first glued-down layer. The visible shims behind the barn openings should be glued so their bottom edges extend under the landform pieces of Layer 2. (See Fig. 5.10-9.)

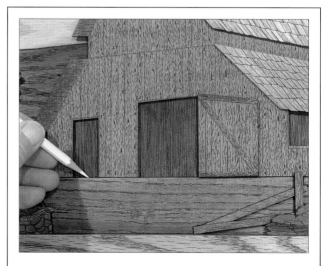

Fig. 5.10-9: Shims glued behind barn.

PROJECT NO. 11
SERENITY

Fig. 5.11-1: The covered bridge is always popular, especially when it has individual shingles and a segmented background.

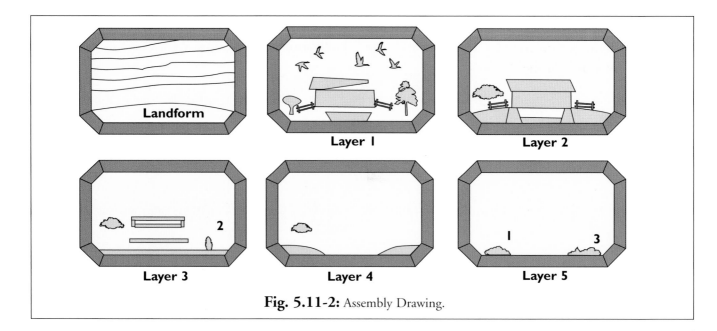

Fig. 5.11-2: Assembly Drawing.

To make Project No. 11, Serenity, Fig. 5.11-1 on page 93, first make the frame and segmented background. (Refer to Frame Styles, Fig. 1-3 on page 11 and Segmented Backgrounds, Fig. 2-6 on page 18.) Paint the background sky pieces in graduated tones of blue, and paint the landform a deep green.

Review Assembly Drawing, Fig. 5.11-2, above, to familiarize yourself with the layers. Make two identical Pierced Cutting pieces of the bridge. (See Fig. 5.11-3 at right.)

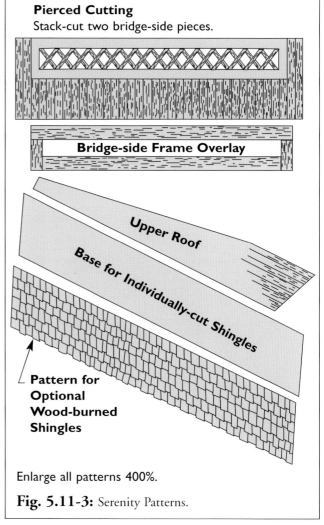

Pierced Cutting
Stack-cut two bridge-side pieces.

Bridge-side Frame Overlay

Upper Roof

Base for Individually-cut Shingles

Pattern for Optional Wood-burned Shingles

Enlarge all patterns 400%.

Fig. 5.11-3: Serenity Patterns.

Begin by selecting vertically grained oak or mahogany. Wood-burn the board lines and optional texturing details. Finish with a dark brown or deep gray stain. Cut the Bridge-side Frame and Bridge-bottom Overlay pieces. Cut the lower-shingle edge for the wood-burned roof option or make the base for applying the individually cut shingles, using the Serenity Patterns, Fig. 5.11-3 on page 94 and Fig. 5.11-4, below.

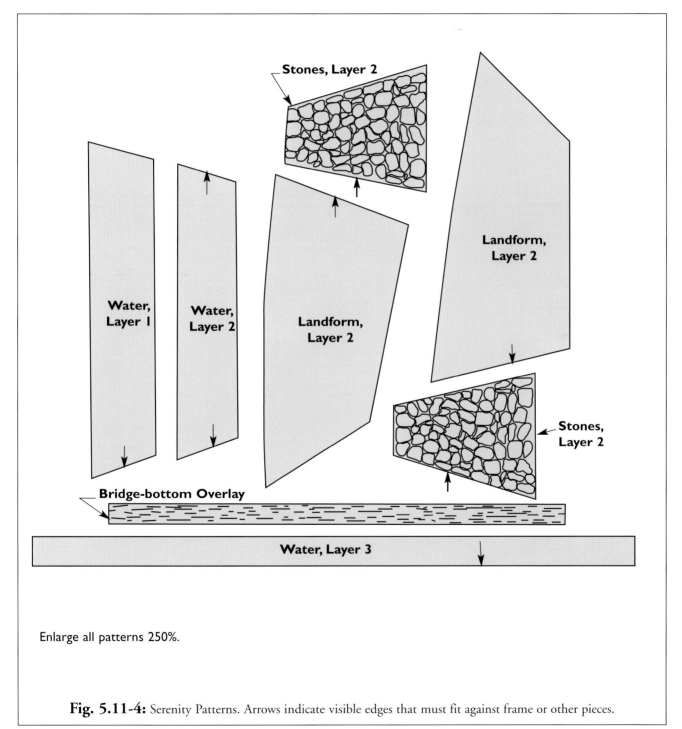

Stones, Layer 2

Landform, Layer 2

Water, Layer I

Water, Layer 2

Landform, Layer 2

Stones, Layer 2

Bridge-bottom Overlay

Water, Layer 3

Enlarge all patterns 250%.

Fig. 5.11-4: Serenity Patterns. Arrows indicate visible edges that must fit against frame or other pieces.

Color the stonework, using six or seven marker colors including reds, browns, grays, and tans. Apply a final light gray with a marker over the stonework to blend.

The roof is either a wood-burned texture or made with individual shingles cut from oak veneer or ½" birch plywood found at hobby stores. Cut the roof shingles, using scissors so they are angled to match the perspective shown in Fig. 5.11-1 on page 93 and Fig. 5.11-3 on page 94. The top row of shingles must be cut to half the length of the other shingles. (See Figs. 5.11-5 through 5.11-9.)

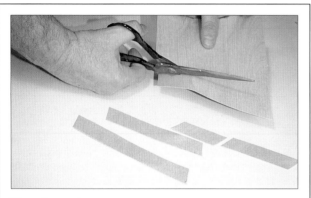

Fig. 5.11-5: Cutting thin veneer into strips that will be cut into individual shingles.

Fig. 5.11-6: Using an angular cut.

Fig. 5.11-7: Cutting the individual shingles.

Fig. 5.11-8: Placing the first row of shingles on a bead of glue with their bottom edges extending slightly over the lower edge of the plywood base.

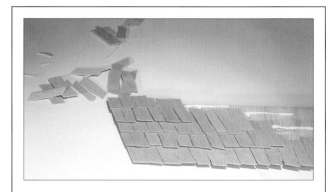

Fig. 5.11-9: A view of the overlapping work.

This project uses the same geese as the Back to the Garden project, on page 86. (Refer to Back to the Garden Patterns, Fig. 5.10-6 on page 91 and Painting the Small Geese on pages 34–36.) The trees and fence are also made and colored essentially the same as those in the Back to the Garden project. (Refer to Back to the Garden, page 92, and see Fig. 5.11-10 on page 97.)

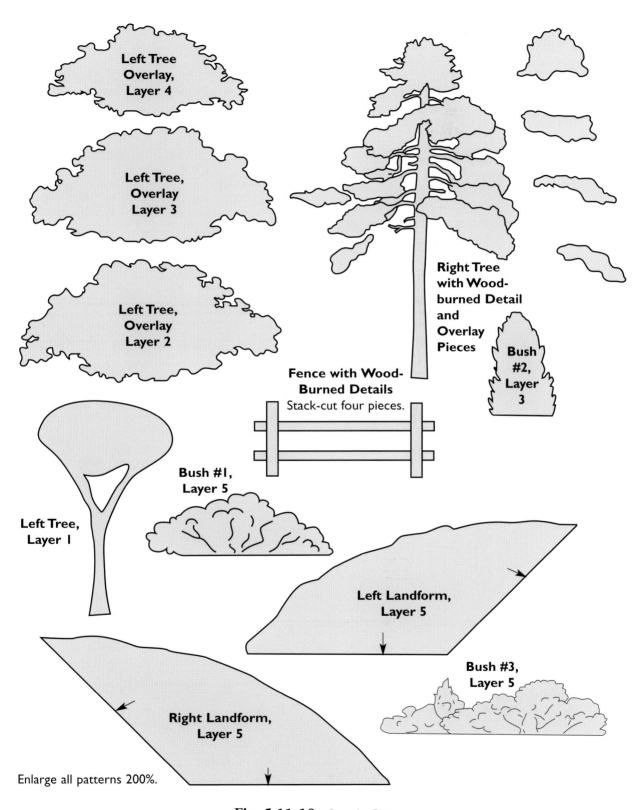

Fig. 5.11-10: Serenity Patterns.

Assemble the wooden bridge as a single unit. The bridge back side piece is positioned laterally approximately ¾" to the left of the front piece, at the same level as the front side piece. By off-setting the two side pieces, the detail of the back side piece is visible through the fretted openings.(See Figs. 5.11-11 through 5.11-13.)

Fig. 5.11-13: Position the roof piece over the front side piece so the top edge tips or slants toward the background, creating a cavity under the roof.

Fig. 5.11-11: Bridge back side piece.

Fig. 5.11-12: Detail of the back side piece visible through the fretted openings.

The stone pillars and the landform to each side are level to each other and shimmed ⅛". Place the assembled bridge so it rests on the two land-form pieces to each side of it. (See Fig. 5.11-14.)

Fig. 5.11-14: Notice that this photo shows three levels of water pieces.

Both tree trunks and the lower fence pieces on the far side slip under these landform pieces.

The uppermost water piece is longer than visually exposed, thus the ends provide a partial shim under each of the two stone pillars. The middle water piece butts against the stone pillars (Layer 2) and slips under the bottom of the lower water piece, serving as a shim.

PROJECT NO. 12
PRAIRIE WINDMILL

Fig. 5.12-1: The old windmill and water tank.

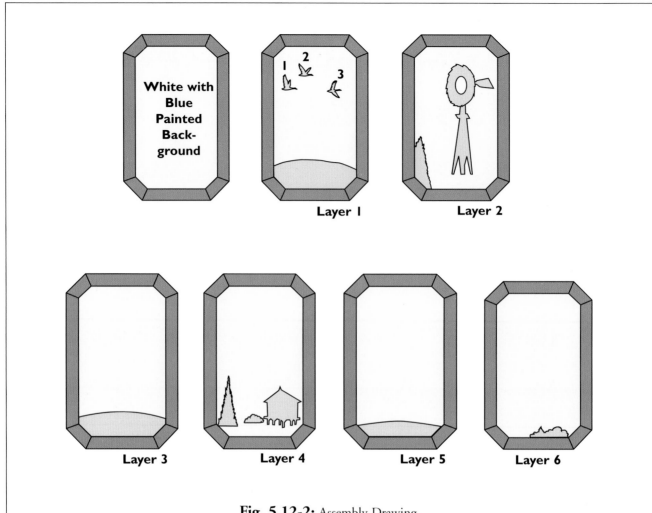

Fig. 5.12-2: Assembly Drawing.

Old windmills are a vanishing sight and affectionately remembered in Project No. 12, Prairie Windmill, Fig. 5.12-1 on page 99. Review Assembly Drawing, Fig. 5.12-2 to familiarize yourself with the layers.

Begin making the vertically rectangular frame, then cut and paint a one-piece background with horizontal grain. (Refer to Frame Styles, Fig. 1-3 on page 11 and Painting One-piece Backgrounds on page 27.)

The windmill consists of many scroll-sawn openings, some wood-burned details, ladder rungs, and brace pieces which are overlaid onto the basic cutout. Use the Prairie Windmill Patterns provided in Figs. 5.12-3 through 5.12-6 on pages 101–104.

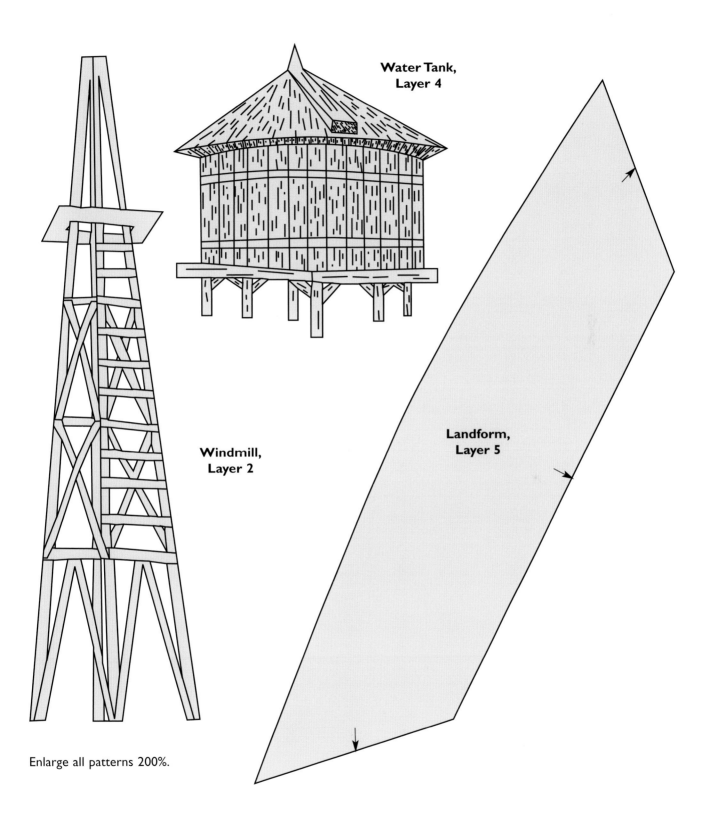

Water Tank, Layer 4

Windmill, Layer 2

Landform, Layer 5

Enlarge all patterns 200%.

Fig. 5.12-3: Prairie Windmill Patterns. Arrows indicate visible edges that must fit against frame or other pieces.

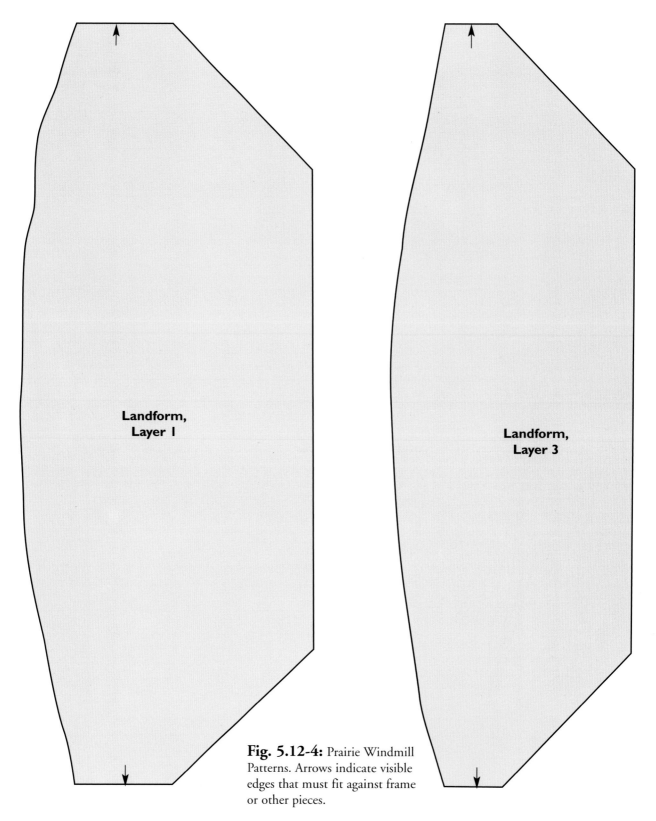

**Landform,
Layer 1**

**Landform,
Layer 3**

Fig. 5.12-4: Prairie Windmill Patterns. Arrows indicate visible edges that must fit against frame or other pieces.

Enlarge all patterns 200%.

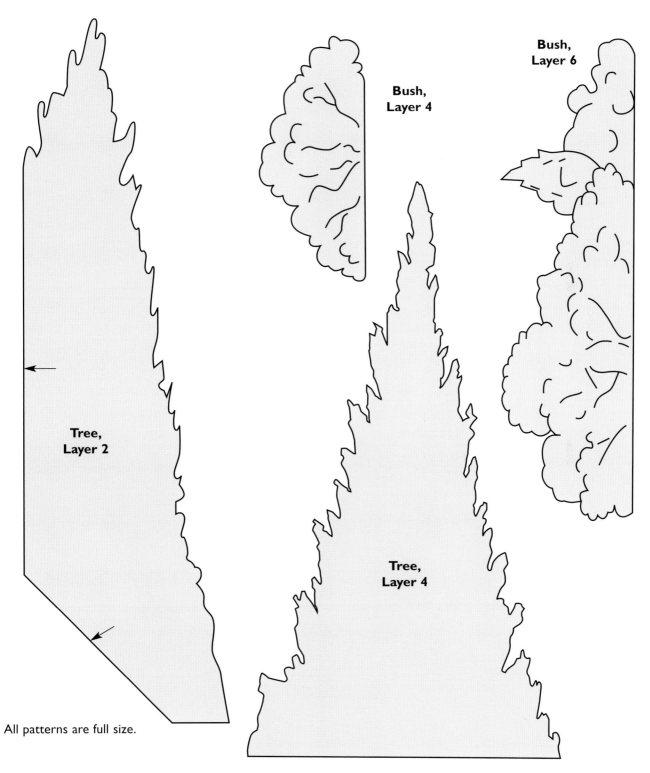

Bush, Layer 4

Bush, Layer 6

Tree, Layer 2

Tree, Layer 4

All patterns are full size.

Fig 5.12-5: Prairie Windmill Patterns.

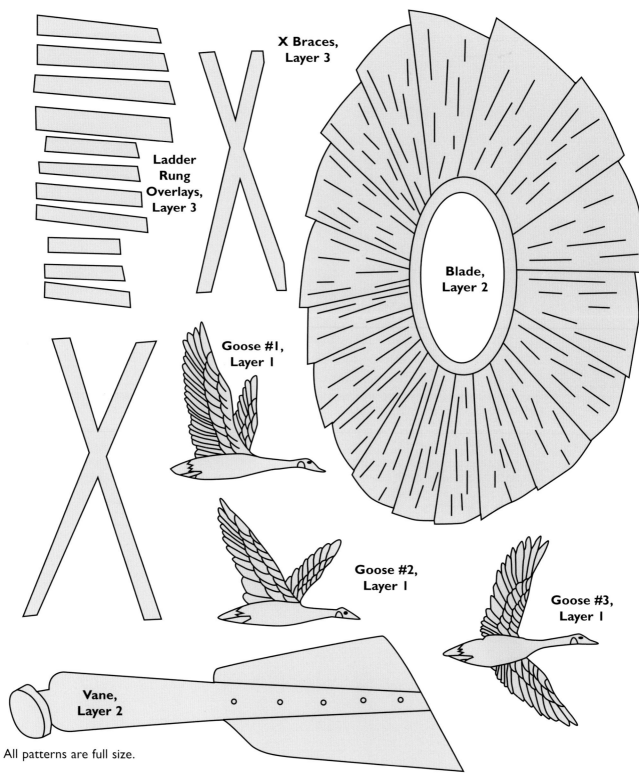

X Braces, Layer 3

Ladder Rung Overlays, Layer 3

Blade, Layer 2

Goose #1, Layer 1

Goose #2, Layer 1

Goose #3, Layer 1

Vane, Layer 2

All patterns are full size.

Fig. 5.12-6: Prairie Windmill Patterns.

104

One small shim is required at the very top of the tower to keep it in the same plane as Layer 2. Making the various layered pieces and coloring them is pretty straightforward. (See Figs. 5.12-7 and 5.12-8.)

Fig. 5.12-7: Notice how lower portions of most pieces slip between the layers of landforms and provide partial shimming.

Fig. 5.12-8: Overlays on the ladder rungs and X braces add dimension.

The ground pieces are muted green with a little brown added. Some shims will be required under the landforms of Layers 3 and 5. Notice how the vane is slipped through the opening from the back of the blades. Consequently, the left end of the vane and the right portion of the blades become elevated. The gluing of the assembly to the background is done with a gap-filling glue at the areas indicated by red arrows in Fig. 5.12-9.

Fig. 5.12-9: The blade and vane assembly is such that the only contacting gluing surfaces are at the arrows. Notice how the wood-burned detail of each blade radiates from the center.

Use glue and small shims as necessary at all contacting points. Color the geese. (Refer to Painting the Small Geese on pages 34–36.) Finally, glue down all parts.

CHAPTER 6
ADVANCED PROJECTS

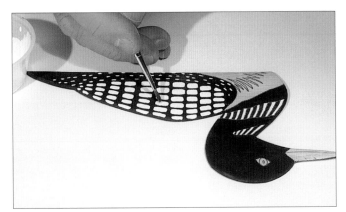

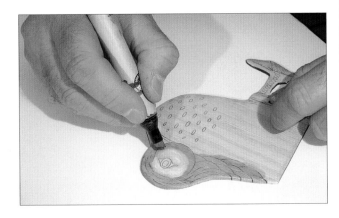

PROJECT No. 13
SETTING UP HOUSEKEEPING

Fig. 6.13-1: Other than wood-burning all of the feather lines on this eagle, this is a relatively easy project to cut, color, and assemble.

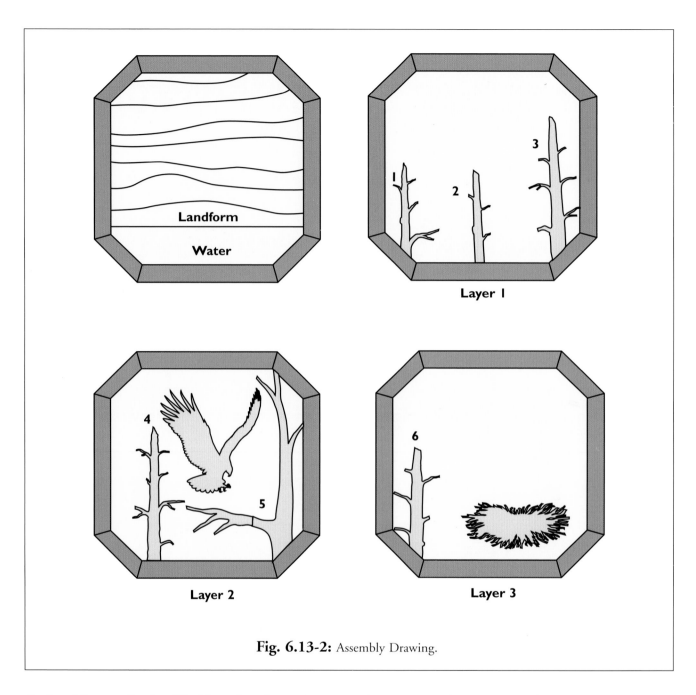

Fig. 6.13-2: Assembly Drawing.

Project No. 13, Setting Up Housekeeping, Fig. 6.13-1 on page 107, uses shims to elevate various parts, giving the wall piece an interesting dimension. Build a square frame and segmented background. (Refer to Frame Styles, Fig. 1-3 on page 11 and Painting Segmented Backgrounds on page 25.) Paint the background sky in graduated tones of blue. Color the bottom water piece blue, and the segment above it green for the shoreline. Glue the background pieces to a backer and mount the assembly to the frame.

Review Assembly Drawing, Fig. 6.13-2, to familiarize yourself with the layers. Use the Setting Up Housekeeping patterns provided in Figs. 6.13-3 through 6.13-5 on pages 109–111.

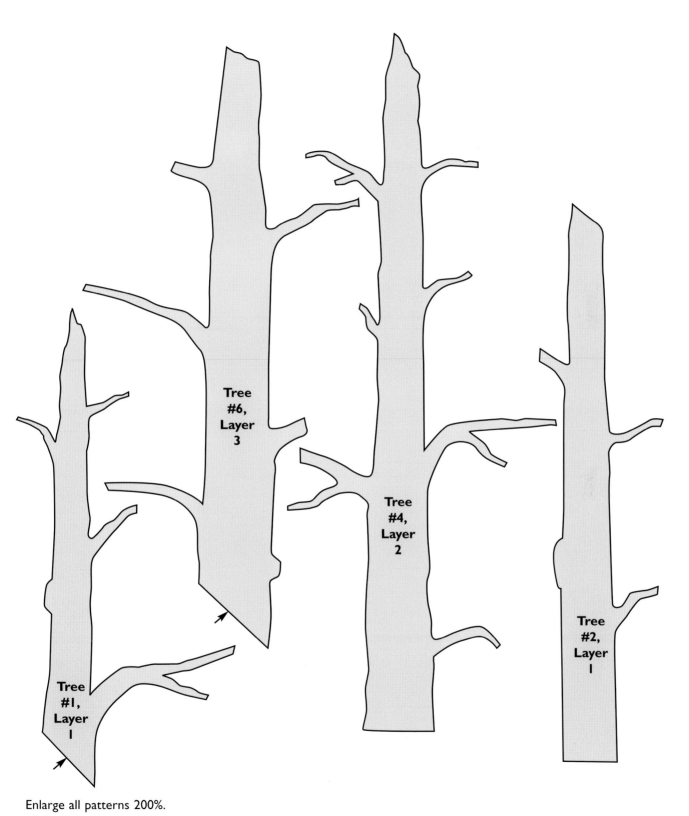

Tree #6, Layer 3

Tree #4, Layer 2

Tree #2, Layer 1

Tree #1, Layer 1

Enlarge all patterns 200%.

Fig. 6.13-3: Setting Up Housekeeping Patterns. Arrows indicate visible edges that must fit against frame.

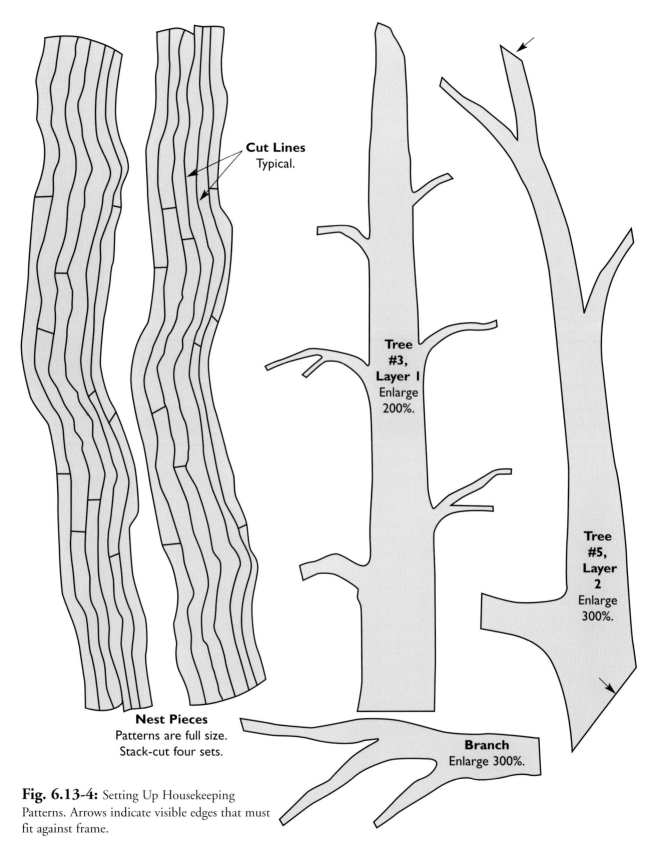

Cut Lines
Typical.

Tree #3, Layer I
Enlarge 200%.

Tree #5, Layer 2
Enlarge 300%.

Branch
Enlarge 300%.

Nest Pieces
Patterns are full size.
Stack-cut four sets.

Fig. 6.13-4: Setting Up Housekeeping
Patterns. Arrows indicate visible edges that must
fit against frame.

**Eagle,
Layer 2**

**Nest Base,
Layer 3**

Up

Enlarge both patterns 200%.

Fig. 6.13-5: Setting Up Housekeeping Patterns.

111

Fit and place the three wood-burned and colored trees of Layer 1. (See Fig. 6.13-6.)

Fig. 6.13-6: Close up of trees in Layers 1–3.

Shim the third tree from the left ⅛". The large tree at the right with the branch for the nest is made in two pieces to save stock and better orient the grain. This tree also is raised with inconspicuously placed ⅛"-thick shims. The tree on the right of Layer 1 will serve as a shim.

Building the nest begins with a single base piece that is a combination of scroll-sawn and wood-burned definition lines. (See Fig. 6.13-7, below, and refer to Fig. 6.13-5 on page 111.)

Fig. 6.13-7: Entire nest glued in place.

Saw out and round over the edges of the various pieces before staining them a deep gray. Glue down the strips in a random pattern with an effort to make it appear as realistic as possible. Build up the central area so the nest has more thickness than at its outer edges. It would be very helpful to refer to a photo of a real eagle's nest.

The eagle requires good wood-burning and coloration of the talons, beak, and eye. Otherwise, the eagle is easily finished, using gray markers. (See Figs. 6.13-8 and 6.13-9.)

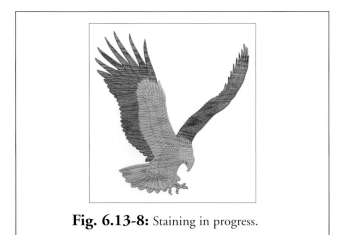

Fig. 6.13-8: Staining in progress.

Fig. 6.13-9: Completed eagle.

The darker areas of the eagle are obtained with the application of a second or third coat. The eagle requires small ⅛"-thick shims to elevate it from the background.

MORNING STRETCH

Fig. 6.14-1: The profound coloring of the mallards is achieved using acrylic paint and markers.

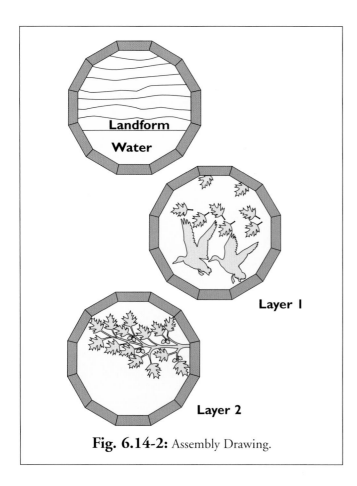

Fig. 6.14-2: Assembly Drawing.

Leaves
Stack-
cut 6–7
of each.

Acorns
Stack-
cut 4
of each.

Enlarge all patterns 200%.

Fig. 6.14-3: Morning Stretch Patterns.

Project No. 14, Morning Stretch, Fig. 16.14-1 on page 113, is certain to attract everyone's attention. The project features a round frame and segmented background. (Refer to Frame Styles, Fig. 1-4 on page 12 and Segmented Backgrounds, Fig. 2-7 on page 19.)

Review Assembly Drawing, Fig. 6.14-2, to familiarize yourself with the layers. Cut out Fig. 6.14-3 at right, and Fig. 6.14-4 on page 115. Stack-cut 6–7 layers of each leaf pattern on the scroll saw. About 25 leaves are required. (Refer to Patterns, Layout, and Cutting Layers on pages 31–32.)

Note: The Leaves in Fig. 6.14-3 are different sizes and have stems that curve in different directions. Also, the leaf stems are tapered and can be cut off at any point to match the cut width of the branch to which it will be connected.

Coloring the Mallards. The wood-burned definition lines of the mallards make distinct color separations and also provide feather texturing on both birds. (See Fig. 6.14-4. on page 115.)

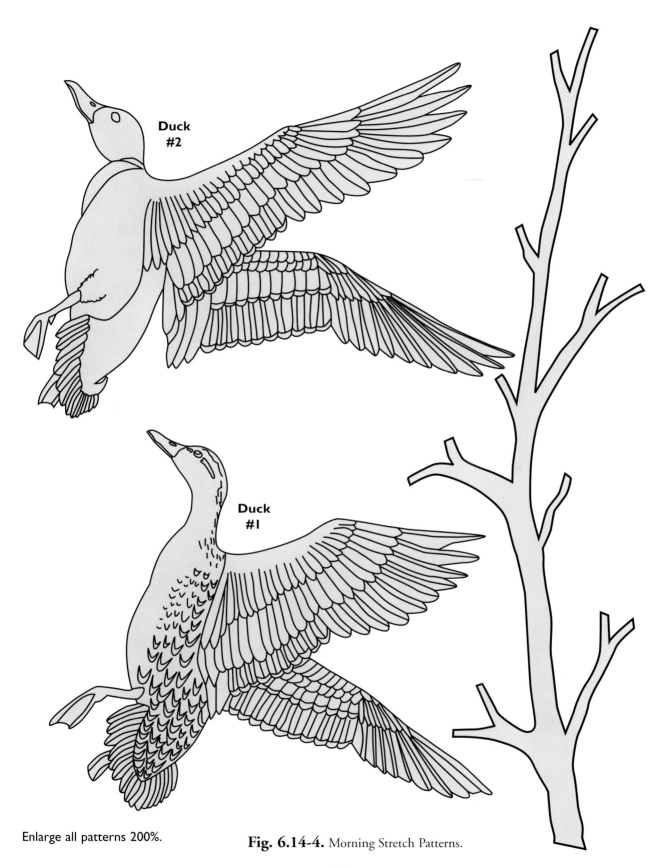

Duck #2

Duck #1

Enlarge all patterns 200%.

Fig. 6.14-4. Morning Stretch Patterns.

115

The mallards are finished with an acrylic white-wash and markers. Outline the feather tips with an ultrafine black marker. Apply brown body color over black defined areas to blend the black with the brown. For the male, Duck #2, make the green back darker by applying several coats. Paint the mallards' eyes black, and paint the white areas with acrylic appropriately thinned with water. The wood-burned feather outlines should still be visible through the white.(See Figs. 6.14-5 through 6.14-9.)

Fig. 6.14-7: Applying brown over the black defined areas of Duck #1.

Fig. 6.14-5: Wood-burning detail lines.

Fig. 6.14-8: Applying green to Duck #2.

Fig. 6.14-6: Coloring the female with markers.

Fig. 6.14-9: Close-up showing wood-burned feather outlines visible through white of wing and tail.

Coloring the Leaves. The reddish tip and the edge blending of the leaves should be done one at a time.

Paint all the leaves (not the stems) with a mixture of 20:80 yellow-gold acrylic and water. Wipe off the excess. When about 95% dry, apply full-strength red acrylic paint to the tips and allow it to partially dry for only a minute or two. (See Fig. 6.14-10.)

Fig. 6.14-10: Applying fall colors to an oak leaf.

Using an old cotton cloth, blend the red paint for the leaf tips into the yellow-gold areas. (See Fig. 6.14-11.)

Fig. 6.14-11: Blending red leaf tip paint into yellow-gold areas.

Use a clean portion of the cloth for blending each leaf. Do not forget to cover and blend in the edge of each leaf.

Glue a few very narrow ⅛"-thick shims to the back of the branch. Additional support to the branch will be provided by six leaves that will be placed under the branch. Place these leaves so the ends of their stems are hidden by the branch.

The leaves of Layer 2 will connect directly to the ends of the branches. Cut the stems of the leaves to match the width where it connects to the branch. Most, if not all, of the leaves of Layer 2 will require a shim. Cut the leaves to fit against the frame and fill in open areas.

Place the acorns in pairs where the leaf stems meet the branch. Use tiny shims as necessary. (See Fig. 6.14-12.)

Fig. 6.14-12: Transition of leaf stems to branch and two acorns placed where stem meets branch.

Place mallards so their wing tips are partially overlapped with several leaves as shown in Fig. 6.14-13.

Fig. 6.14-13: Close-up of mallards glued directly to background with layers of leaves overlapping the wing tips.

PROJECT NO. 15
RACING THE WIND

Fig. 6.15-1: A buck on the "move" could not look more realistic.

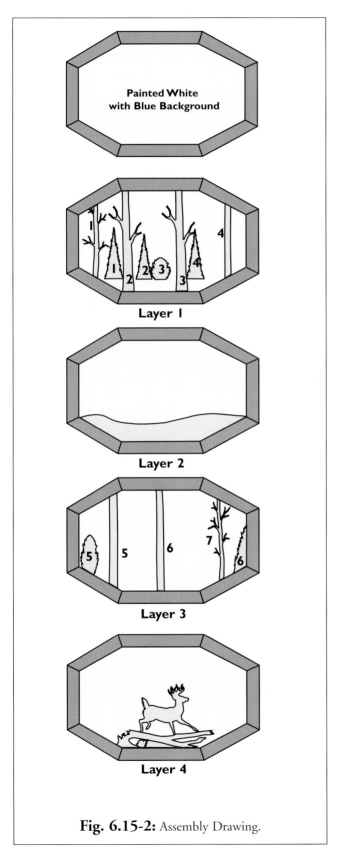

Fig. 6.15-2: Assembly Drawing.

Project No. 15, Racing the Wind, Fig. 5.15-1 on page 118, is built upon a painted background within an oval frame. (Refer to Frame Styles, Fig. 1-4 on page 12 and Coloring One-piece Background Segments on pages 27–28.)

Review Assembly Drawing, Fig. 6.15-2, at left, to familiarize yourself with the layers. Cut out all pieces using the Racing the Wind Patterns in Fig. 6.15-3, below, and Figs. 6.15-4 through 6.15-6 on pages 120–122.

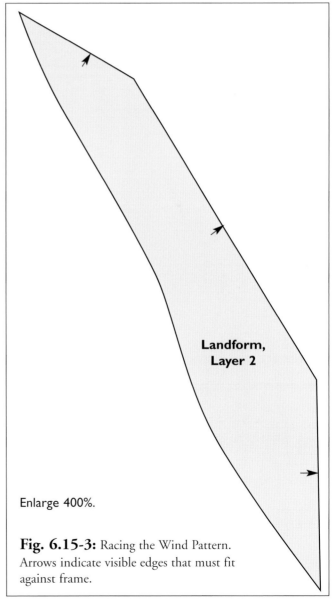

Enlarge 400%.

Fig. 6.15-3: Racing the Wind Pattern. Arrows indicate visible edges that must fit against frame.

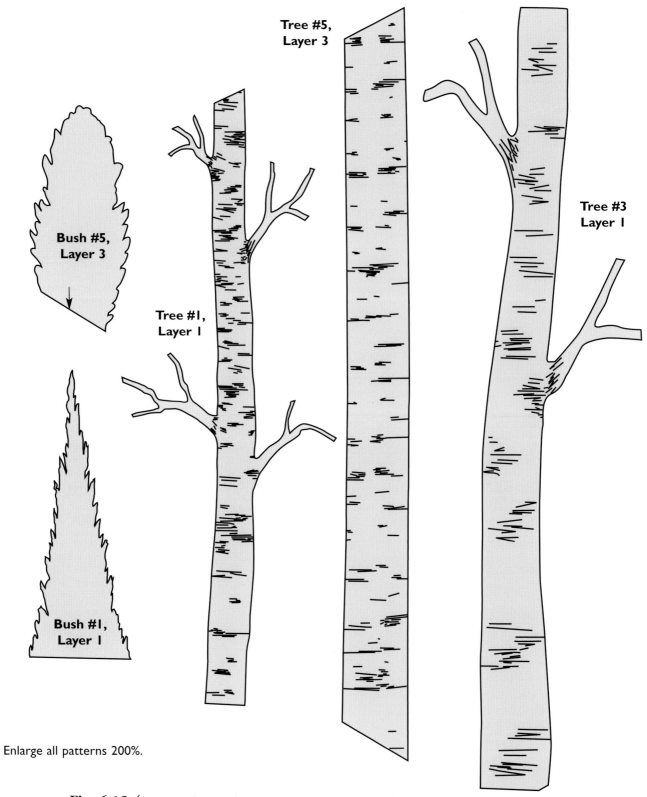

Bush #5, Layer 3

Tree #5, Layer 3

Tree #1, Layer 1

Tree #3 Layer 1

Bush #1, Layer 1

Enlarge all patterns 200%.

Fig. 6.15-4: Racing the Wind Patterns. Arrows indicate visible edges that must fit against frame.

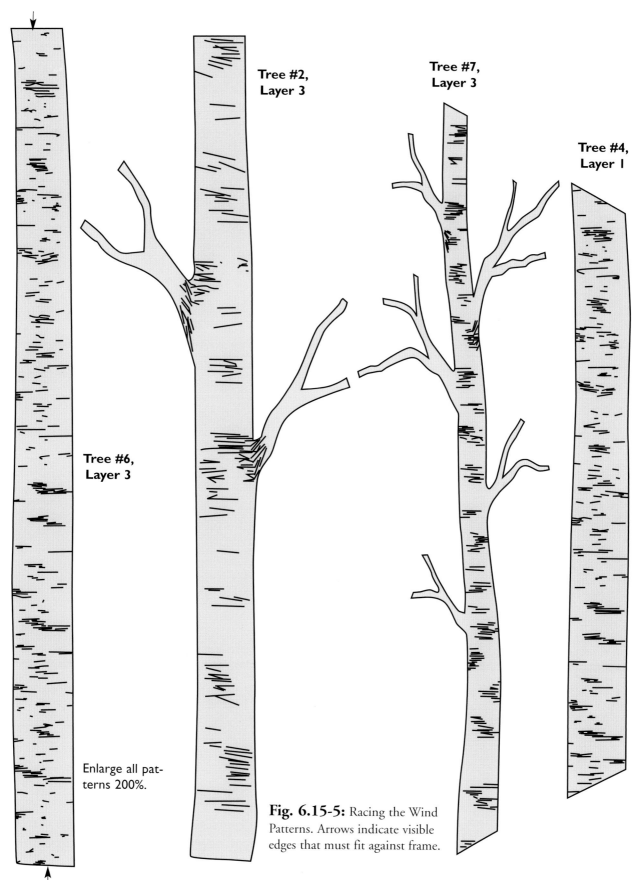

Tree #2, Layer 3

Tree #7, Layer 3

Tree #4, Layer 1

Tree #6, Layer 3

Enlarge all patterns 200%.

Fig. 6.15-5: Racing the Wind Patterns. Arrows indicate visible edges that must fit against frame.

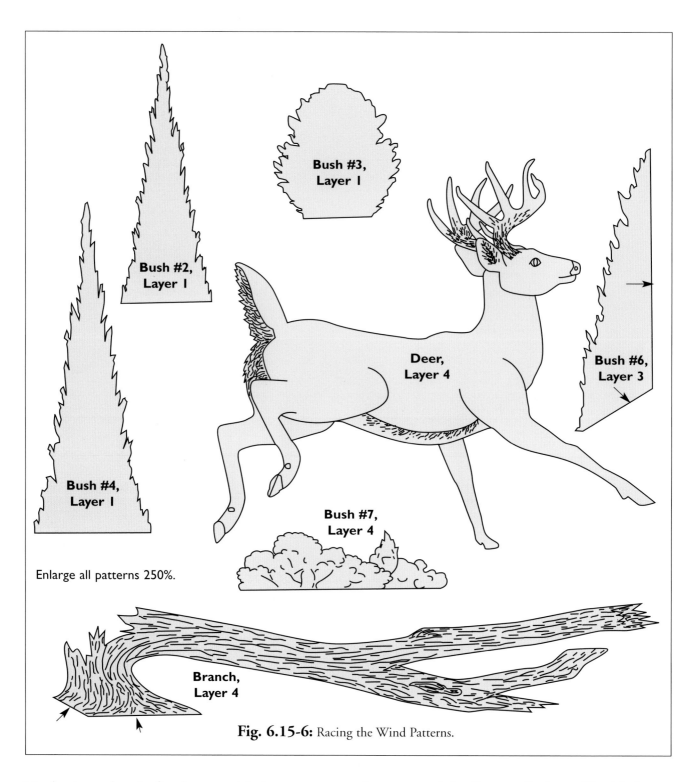

Fig. 6.15-6: Racing the Wind Patterns.

Bush #3, Layer 1

Bush #2, Layer 1

Bush #4, Layer 1

Enlarge all patterns 250%.

Deer, Layer 4

Bush #6, Layer 3

Bush #7, Layer 4

Branch, Layer 4

Use horizontal grain for the seven birch trees. Rotary-cut red oak for the trees can be used but birch may be better. Copy as much detail on the fallen tree as you feel necessary, then wood-burn the suggested detail onto all pieces. The birch trees are given a wash of 50:50 white acrylic and water and applied so the wood-burned lines are visible.

Finish and color the deer. (Refer to Making and Coloring Deer on pages 36–37 and see Figs. 6.15-6 through 6.15-7, below.)

Fig. 6.15-6: Colored buck. Notice the vertical grain and transparent whitewashed areas, allowing wood-burned details to show through.

Fig. 6.15-7: Close-up of head details.

Note: Most of the birch trees will need to be cut to fit at their top ends. The bottoms will be covered. The trees in Layer 3 will require top shims or can be glued directly to the upper background. (See Fig. 6.15-8.)

Fig. 6.15-8: Notice how the bottoms of the first and third trees from the left serve as partial shims for the landform.

A ⅛"-thick shim provides gluing support under the deer. The buck is placed so his front legs are to the far side of the fallen tree and the rear legs are on the near side. (See Fig. 6.15-9.)

Fig. 6.15-9: Notice how the center birch tree is glued to the landform layer at the bottom and to the background at the top.

PROJECT No. 16
OCTOBER IN THE WOODS

Fig. 6.16-1: Another version of a deer scene somewhat similar to the Racing the Wind project on page 118.

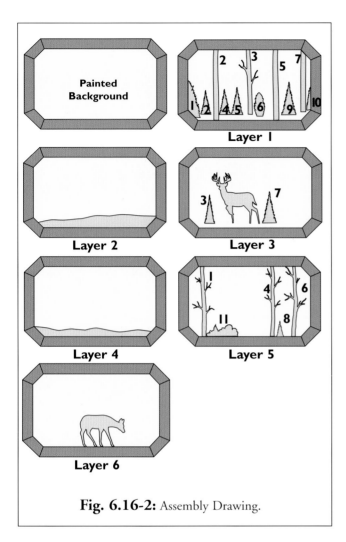

Fig. 6.16-2: Assembly Drawing.

Project No. 16, October in the Woods, Fig. 6.16-1 on page 124, involves similar components and employs exactly the same techniques as Project 15, Racing the Wind, on pages 118–123, but creates a setting that is much more dimensional. This project has a rectangular frame and a white-and-blue painted background. (Refer to Frame Styles, Fig. 1-3 on page 11 and Painting One-piece Backgrounds on page 27.)

Review Assembly Drawing, Fig. 6.16-2, to familiarize yourself with the layers.

Use the patterns in Fig. 6.16-3 at right and Figs. 6.16-4 through 6.16-7 on pages 126–129.

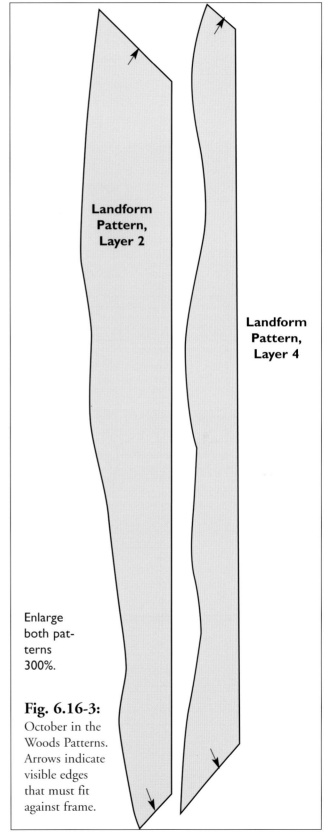

Landform Pattern, Layer 2

Landform Pattern, Layer 4

Enlarge both patterns 300%.

Fig. 6.16-3: October in the Woods Patterns. Arrows indicate visible edges that must fit against frame.

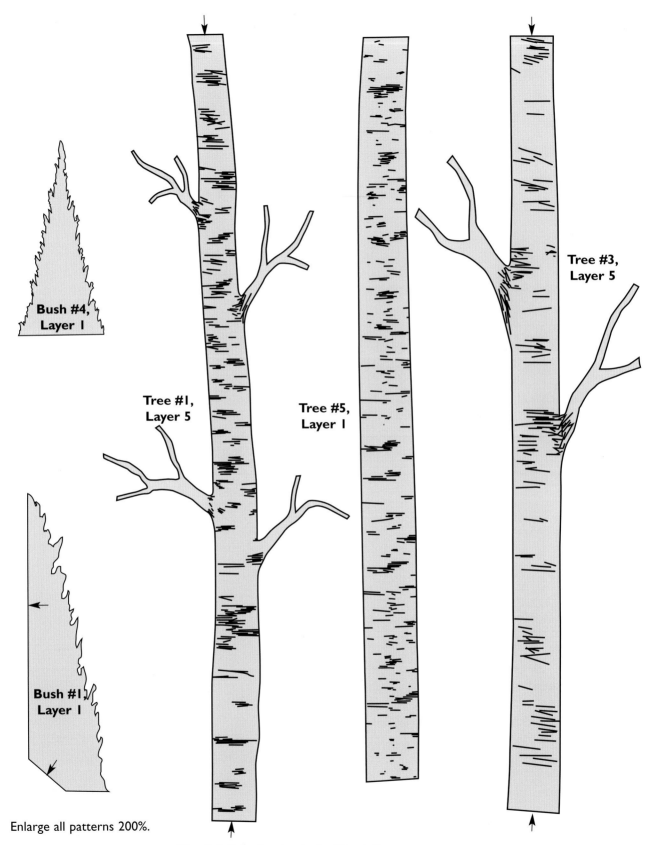

Bush #4,
Layer 1

Bush #1,
Layer 1

Tree #1,
Layer 5

Tree #5,
Layer 1

Tree #3,
Layer 5

Enlarge all patterns 200%.

Fig. 6.16-4: October in the Woods Patterns.

126

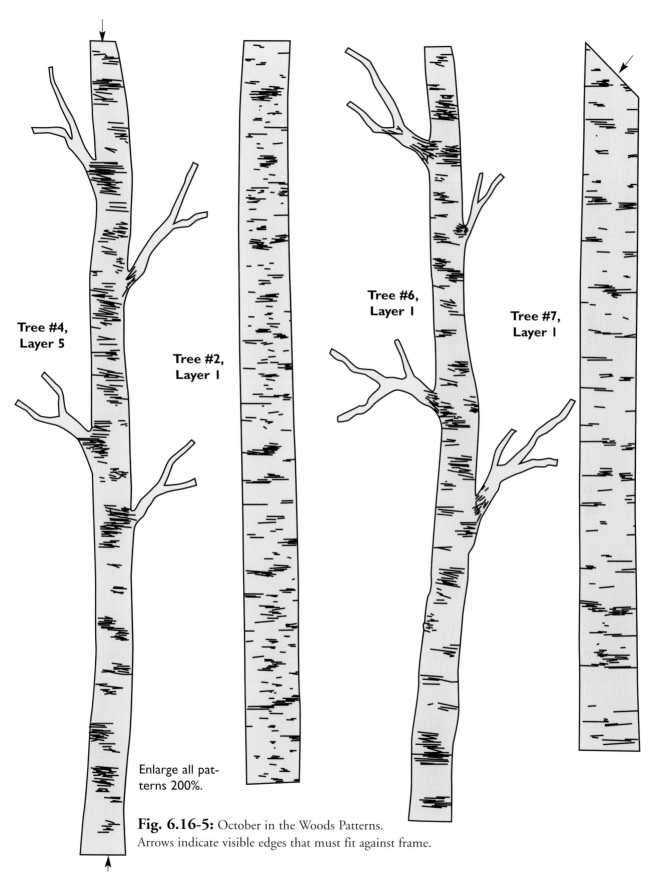

Tree #4, Layer 5

Tree #2, Layer 1

Tree #6, Layer 1

Tree #7, Layer 1

Enlarge all patterns 200%.

Fig. 6.16-5: October in the Woods Patterns.
Arrows indicate visible edges that must fit against frame.

Bush #11, Layer 5

Buck, Layer 3

Bush #3, Layer 3

Bush #2, Layer 1

Doe, Layer 5

Bush #7, Layer 3

Enlarge all patterns 200%.

Fig. 6.16-6: October in the Woods Patterns. Arrows indicate visible edges that must fit against frame.

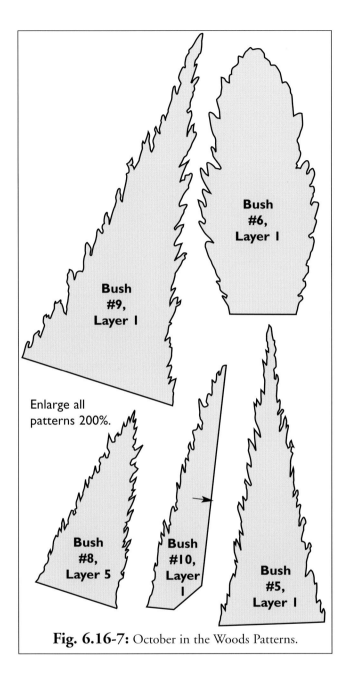

Fig. 6.16-7: October in the Woods Patterns.

The image contains the following labels: Bush #6, Layer I; Bush #9, Layer I; Bush #8, Layer 5; Bush #10, Layer I; Bush #5, Layer I; Enlarge all patterns 200%.

Trace the bottom frame edges and fit the landforms, then attach the background to the frame. Freehand the irregular curves on the top edges of the landforms or use Fig. 6.16-4 on page 126.

Color the deer. (Refer to Making and Coloring Deer on page 36, and see Figs. 6.16-8 through 6.16-10 at right and 6.16-11 on page 130.)

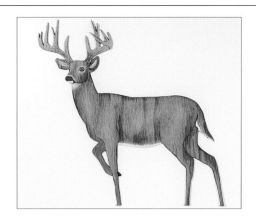

Fig. 6.16-8: Completed buck. Notice the deeper tan color under the chin, belly, and far leg.

Fig. 6.16-9: Close-up of head. Notice the darker brown coloring on the right side of the face and ear.

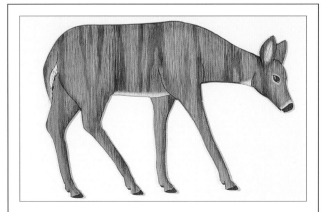

Fig. 6.16-10: Completed doe. Notice the darker coloring along the front edge of the legs.

Fig. 6.16-11: Close-up of blended whites and darker perimeter of near ears, lower and top edges.

Fig. 6.16-12: Layering of birch trees.

Fig. 6.16-13: Feet of the buck tucked under Landform in Layer 4.

The birch trees are cut to fit against the top edge of the frame. Their lower ends will be covered with landforms as will be the hooves of the buck. The three birch trees of Layer 5 with bottoms glued to the Layer 4 landform have their tops either glued directly to the background or over small, ⅛"-thick shims. The feet of the buck tuck under the Landform in Layer 4 and serve as partial shims.(See Figs. 6.16-12 and 6.16-13.)

Some trees may be supported with ⅛"-thick shims and the buck requires one or two ¼"-thick shims. A ⅛"-thick shim is also required between the buck and the doe.

PROJECT No. 17
SPRINGTIME ON THE LAKE

Fig. 6.17-1: Loon family enjoying "Springtime on the Lake."

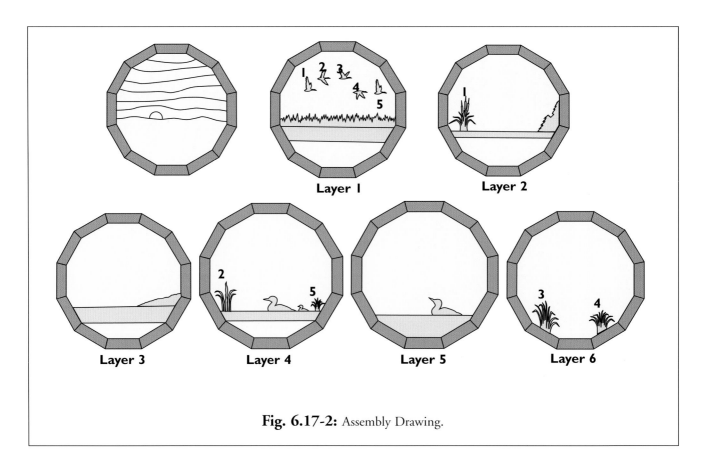

Fig. 6.17-2: Assembly Drawing.

Loon-related art is always popular. This version is no exception and it is one of the best-selling projects. Project No. 17, Springtime on the Lake, Fig. 6.17-1 on page 131, consists of six layers of ⅛"-thick cutouts. Thicker plywood or thick glue lines may add up to more than the ¾"of working space. Using plywood ⅒"-thick is recommended. It may be necessary to thin down some of the layers or begin with a frame thickness greater than ¾". If necessary to reduce the thicknesses, use a thickness planer with the workpieces supported on a plywood carrier. The best way to reduce material thickness is to use a thickness drum sander.

The project features a round frame. (Refer to Frame Styles, Fig. 1-4 on page 12.) The segmented background is drawn freehand or enlarged with a photocopy machine. (Refer to Segmented Backgrounds, Fig. 2-7 on page 19.) The background can either be colored in graduated shades of white-blue or yellow-orange. Both create a dramatic backdrop for the loons and other components. Paint the sun of the red-orange background a vivid, fluorescent yellow-gold. Paint the sun a white color when a blue sky is selected.

Review Assembly Drawing, Fig. 6.17-2 to familiarize yourself with the layers. It is best to cut all four of the water pieces from the same piece of plywood for consistency of color and pattern. Use vertical grain for the tree line and horizontal grain for the water pieces. The cutting details for the water layers and the tree line are given in Fig. 6.17-3 on page 133.

Note: The water piece in Layer 2 is actually a shim and only its very top edge is visible. This edge surface is flush and level to the top edge of the water piece of Layer 3.

132

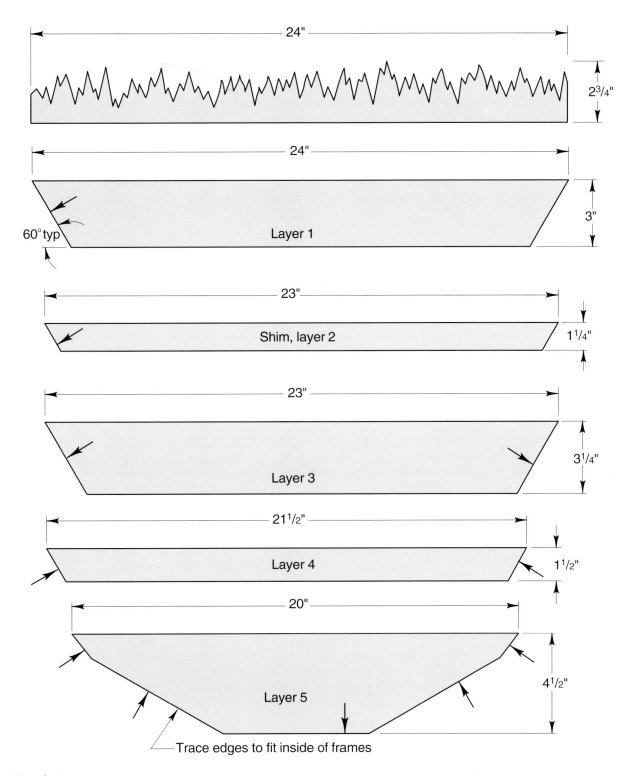

24"

2³/4"

24"

60° typ

Layer 1

3"

23"

Shim, layer 2

1¹/4"

23"

Layer 3

3¹/4"

21¹/2"

Layer 4

1¹/2"

20"

Layer 5

4¹/2"

Trace edges to fit inside of frames

Fig. 6.17-3: Details for the shoreline and water pieces. Draw the shoreline freehand. All dimensions are only approximate. Since frames may vary in size, trace and hand-fit all pieces. Arrows indicate visible edges that must fit against frame.

All of the dimensions given are only approximate and suggestive. Before attaching the background and backer to the frame, trace and fit all water pieces to the inside on the frame.

Cut out all other parts, using patterns in Fig. 6.17-4, below, and Figs. 6.17-5 through 6.17-6 on pages 135–136.

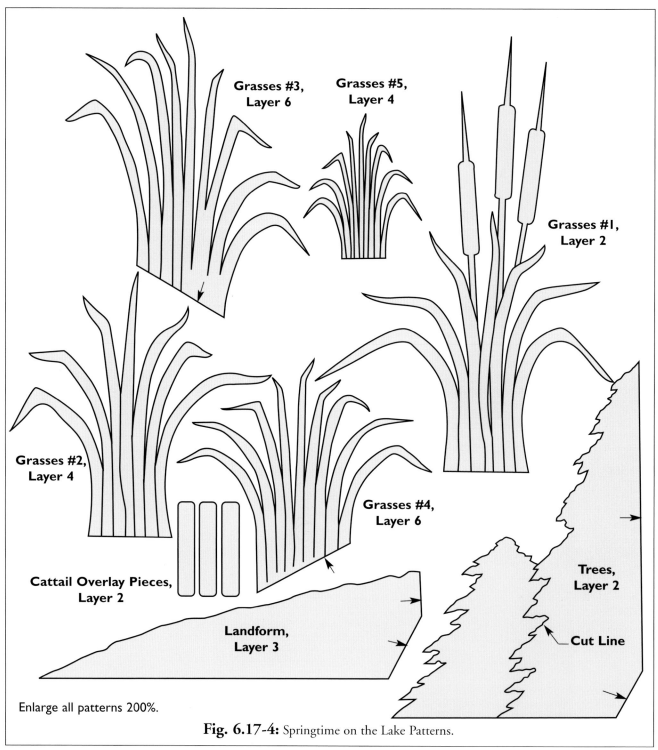

Fig. 6.17-4: Springtime on the Lake Patterns.

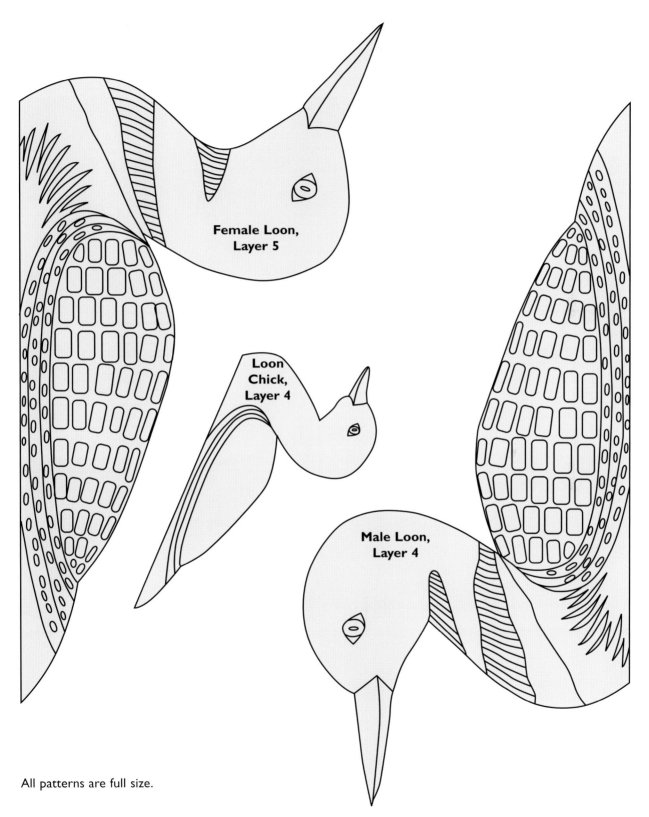

Female Loon, Layer 5

Loon Chick, Layer 4

Male Loon, Layer 4

All patterns are full size.

Fig. 6.17-5: Springtime on the Lake Patterns.

135

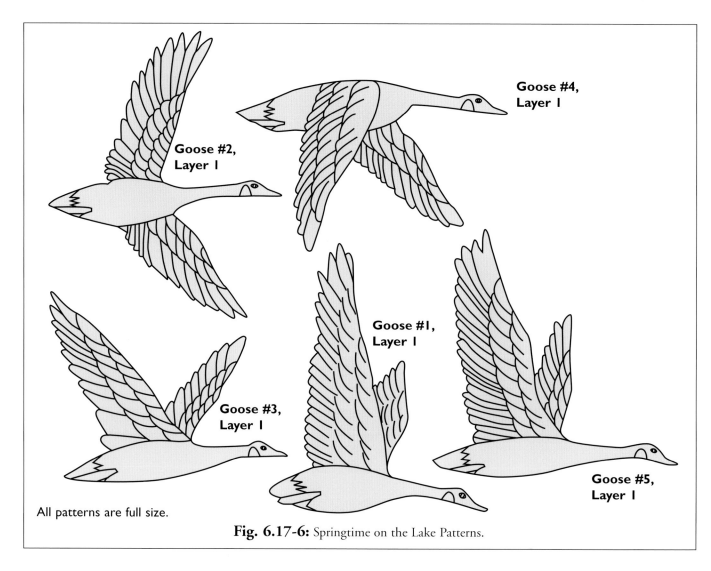

Goose #4, Layer 1

Goose #2, Layer 1

Goose #1, Layer 1

Goose #3, Layer 1

Goose #5, Layer 1

All patterns are full size.

Fig. 6.17-6: Springtime on the Lake Patterns.

Round over the various parts as appropriate. Refer to Creating Cattails on page 33 for more information about making two-layer cattails. These small cattails are very fragile, so use care.

Refer to Painting the Small Geese on page 34 for painting the five small geese. Set them aside and glue them in place as the final step.

Painting the Loons. The painting of white over deep gray or black coloring is a little tricky. First, paint everything a dark charcoal gray (almost black) except the bill and eyes. Now, spray a thin coat of acrylic clear finish over the dark color. This acts as a sealer and will prevent the black paint from bleeding into the white and making a muddy gray mess. Very small "dots" are best painted using a round-pointed toothpick. The baby chick is painted a dark brown. Study Figs. 6.17-7 through 6.17-10 on page 137.

136

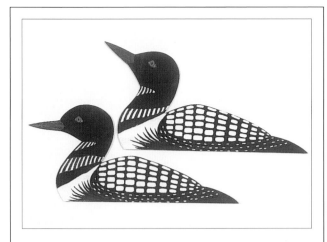

Fig. 6.17-7: Painted loons, ready for assembly.

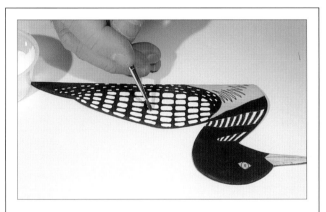

Fig. 6.17-8: Painting white over dark gray after sealer is sprayed over surface.

Fig. 6.17-9: Adding "dots" with a round-pointed toothpick.

Fig. 6.17-10: Painted loons glued against top edges of Layers 4 and 5.

Paint the water layers blue. Remember to paint the tree line edges and the top edges of the various pieces because they are visible. The two trees of Layer 2 sit on ⅛" shims.

Assembly. The small landform piece of Layer 3 covers the bottoms of the trees. Place the grasses, one loon, and the chick of Layer 4. Add the second loon in Layer 5 (See Fig. 6.17-11.)

Fig. 6.17-11: Close-up showing cattails and grasses butting against top edges of Layers 3 and 4.

Add the grasses to complete Layer 6. Cut, fit and glue down the final clumps of grasses. Finally, glue the small geese to the sky background.

PROJECT No. 18
ALWAYS ON GUARD

Fig. 6.18-1: This loon project involves many of the same techniques used in previous loon projects.

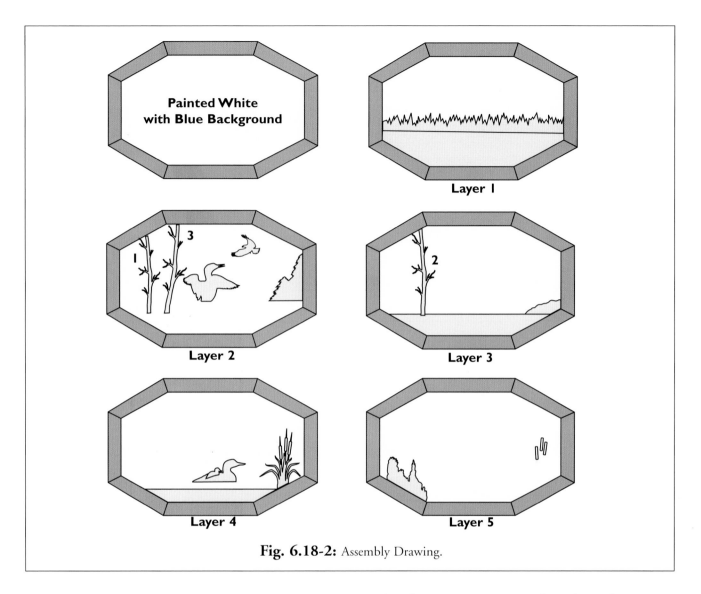

Painted White with Blue Background

Layer 1

Layer 2

Layer 3

Layer 4

Layer 5

Fig. 6.18-2: Assembly Drawing.

Project No. 18, Always on Guard, Fig. 6.18-1 on page 138, depicts a Northern Loon ready to protect its chick from a hungry eagle. The picture is showcased in an oval frame with a painted background. (Refer to Frame Styles, Fig. 1-4 on page 12 and Painting One-piece Backgrounds on page 27.) Review the Springtime on the Lake project on pages 131–137 because many of the elements and techniques are very similar. Also refer to Painting the Loons on page 136 for directions on painting the loons.

Review Assembly Drawing, Fig. 6.18-2 to familiarize yourself with the layers. Use the Always on Guard Patterns in Figs. 6.18-3 through 6.18-6 on pages 140–143.

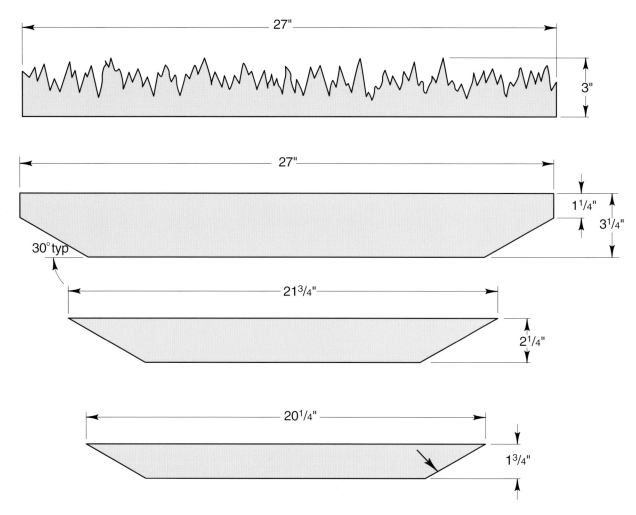

Fig. 6.18-3: Always on Guard Patterns. Arrows indicate visible edges that must fit against the frame.

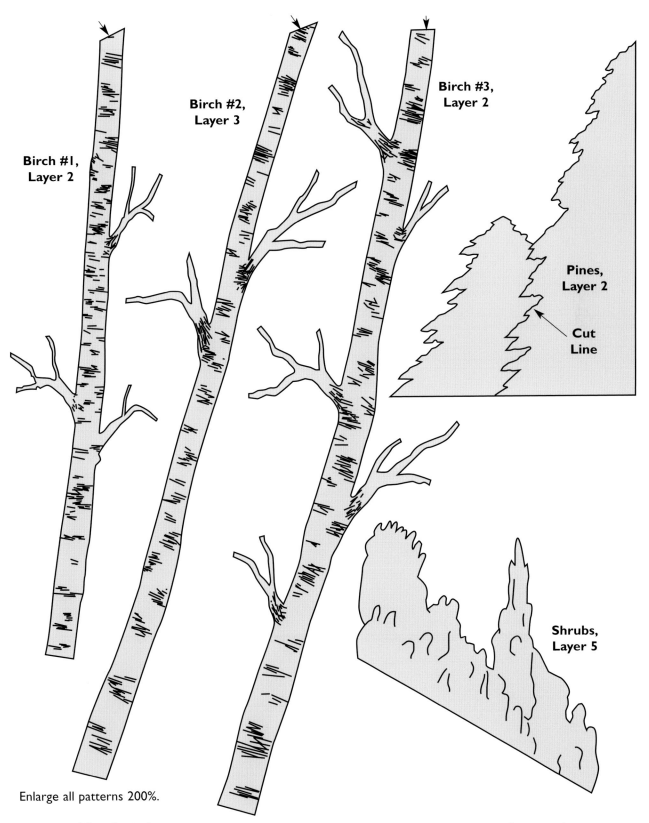

Birch #1,
Layer 2

Birch #2,
Layer 3

Birch #3,
Layer 2

Pines,
Layer 2

Cut
Line

Shrubs,
Layer 5

Enlarge all patterns 200%.

Fig. 6.18-4: Always on Guard Patterns. Arrows indicate visible edges that must fit against frame.

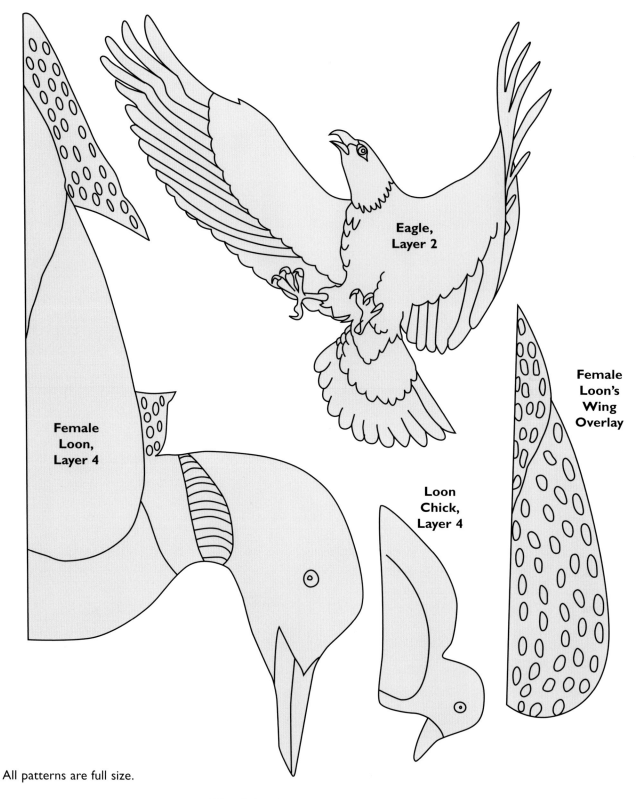

Female
Loon,
Layer 4

Eagle,
Layer 2

Female
Loon's
Wing
Overlay

Loon
Chick,
Layer 4

All patterns are full size.

Fig. 6.18-5: Always on Guard Patterns.

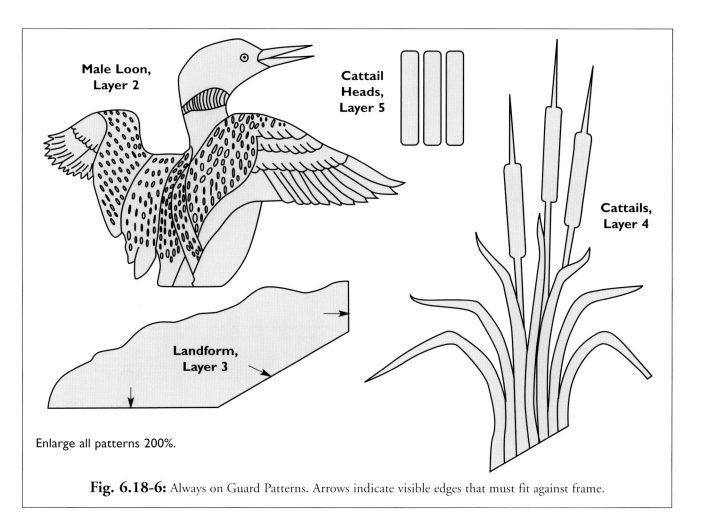

Male Loon, Layer 2

Cattail Heads, Layer 5

Cattails, Layer 4

Landform, Layer 3

Enlarge all patterns 200%.

Fig. 6.18-6: Always on Guard Patterns. Arrows indicate visible edges that must fit against frame.

Cut out all parts and wood-burn the detail lines for texture and painting. Notice that the female loon and chick are three parts. The chick fits into a pocket on its mother's back and a wing piece is laid over the body. Notice the unpainted area. (See Figs. 6.18-7, right, and 6.18-8 on page 144.)

Fig. 6.18-7: Completed loons.

Fig. 6.18-8: Close-up of chick riding on its mother's back.

Refer to Creating Cattails on page 33 for tips and options about making two-piece cattails. They are very fragile and need to be made and handled with care. The eagle is simply painted a deep gray-brown and white. (See Fig. 6.18-9.)

Fig. 6.18-9: Close-up of eagle detail.

Fig. 6.18-10: Close-up of two outside birch trees.

Fig. 6.18-11: Layering of the loons.

The assembly is relatively simple. The two outside birch trees are placed on Layer 2 and the center tree is placed on Layer 3. The male loon is placed first on Layer 2. The loon with the chick is placed on Layer 3, butting against the top edge of Layer 4. A ⅛"-thick shim is placed under the eagle. (See Figs. 6.18-10 and 6.18-11.)

144

PROJECT No. 19
TWO BUMPS ON A LOG

Fig. 6.19-1: Coloring the wood ducks presents the major challenge of this project.

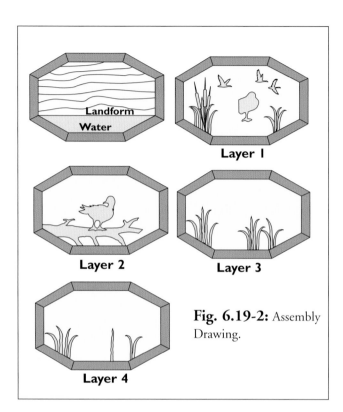

Fig. 6.19-2: Assembly Drawing.

Scroll-sawing and assembly are the easy tasks involved in making Project No. 19, Two Bumps on a Log, Fig. 6.19-1 on page 145. The challenge is to simulate the realistic coloring on this pair of wood-duck cutouts as closely as possible. This project is made with an oval frame and a segmented background. (Refer to Frame Styles, Fig. 1-4 on page 12 and Segmented Backgrounds, Fig. 2-8 on page 20.)

Review Assembly Drawing, Fig. 6.19-2, to familiarize yourself with the layers. Cut out the patterns, using Fig. 6.19-3 at right and Fig. 6.19-4 on page 147.

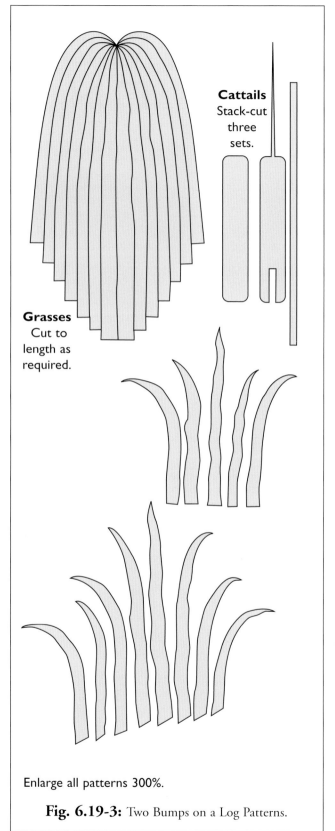

Cattails Stack-cut three sets.

Grasses Cut to length as required.

Enlarge all patterns 300%.

Fig. 6.19-3: Two Bumps on a Log Patterns.

**Geese,
Layer 1**
Enlarge 150%.

**Wood Duck,
Layer 1**
Enlarge 300%.

**Wood Duck,
Layer 2**
Enlarge 300%.

Log, Layer 2
Enlarge 400%.

Fig. 6.19-4: Two Bumps on a Log Patterns.

Refer to Creating Cattails on page 33 for helpful information about making the cattails. About 27–30 pieces of grass are required. Since they are various lengths, it is best to cut off the bottoms as you place and fit each piece into the picture.

The male wood duck and the log are at the same level (Layer 2) and must be cut so the feet fit into the top edge of the log. (See Fig. 6.19-13 on page 149.) Cut the log profile carefully first. Next, use the log cutout as a pattern to cut the exact matching profile along the bottom of the duck's

feet. Cut out and color all other parts. (Refer to Painting the Small Geese on page 34.)

One of the trickier jobs when coloring the wood ducks is to achieve the realistic coloring of the cheek and the blended area around the eye of the female. Make practice tests of the blending colors on scrap before attempting it. Apply a base coat with a light brown marker. Brush white acrylic around the eye and cheek. Blend the white to the basecoat brown color, using a blending marker (a special marker that contains no pigment). Apply some darker brown to the top of the head and lower cheek as shown. Blend with a blending marker or use a very light brown marker as a blender. The completed cheek should appear rounded, almost like a billiard ball. Complete the coloring using shades of brown and white markings. (See Figs. 6.19-5 through 6.19-10.)

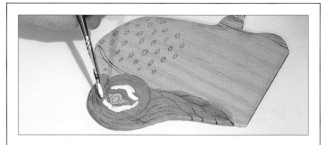

Fig. 6.19-7: Brushing white around eye and cheek.

Fig. 6.19-5: Finished female wood duck, with wood-burned details and blended coloring.

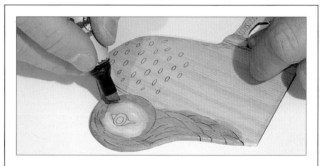

Fig. 6.19-8: Blending white to the base-coat color.

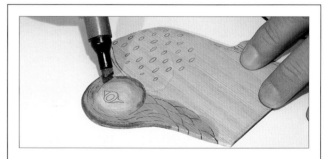

Fig. 6.19-9: Applying darker brown to the top of the head and lower cheek.

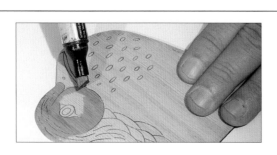

Fig. 6.19-6: Applying light brown base coat around the eye and cheek area.

Fig. 6.19-10: Completed cheek.

Coloring the male is done primarily with markers except for the white acrylic markings which are applied after coloring with the markers is done. Begin with shades of browns and green. (See Figs. 6.19-11 and 6.19-12.)

Fig. 6.19-11: Partially colored male wood duck.

Fig. 6.19-12: Completed male.

Notice the blending of the red-violet to blue on the middle side feathers and the red to a yellowish brown on the chest. These blended areas are all colored using markers.

The assembly is fairly routine. Use very small, inconspicuous shims to support delicate parts. The feet of the male wood duck fit into a matching cut opening of the log, making their surfaces flush to each other. The foot of the female, however, is just slightly behind the log and serves as a partial shim. Cattails made with plywood stems are glued directly to the background. Also, notice that about five pieces of grass are placed with them as the Layer 1. The log and the male wood duck make up Layer 2. (See Figs. 6.19-13 and 6.19-14.)

Fig. 6.19-13: The male duck's feet fit into matching profiles cut out of the log.

Fig. 6.19-14: Cattails made with plywood stems glued directly to the background.

PROJECT NO. 20
FALL PHEASANTS

Fig. 6.20-1: The selection and blending of the male colors are the major challenges of this project.

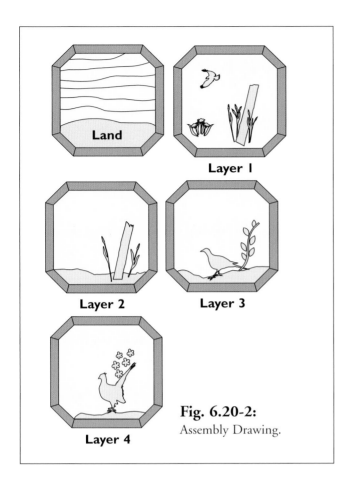

Fig. 6.20-2: Assembly Drawing.

the edges of the top layer well-rounded over. The amount of burned detail is optional. The burned knots give the project more visual appeal. Cut using Fall Pheasant Pattern Fig. 6.20-3.

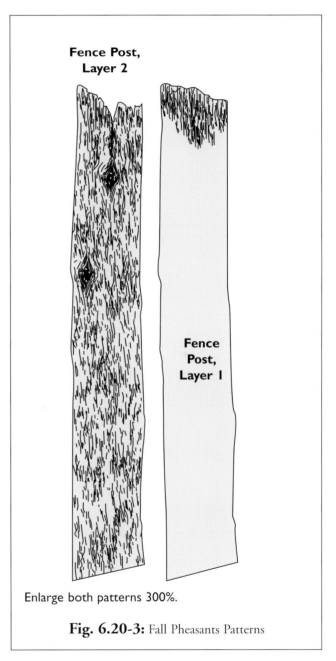

Enlarge both patterns 300%.

Fig. 6.20-3: Fall Pheasants Patterns

Like the wood ducks in Project 19, Two Bumps on a Log, Fig. 6.19-1 on page 145, creating the most realistic coloring possible is the key to the visual intensity of Project No. 20, Fall Pheasants, Fig. 6.20-1 on page 150. It features a square frame and a segmented background. (Refer to Frame Styles, Fig. 1-3 on page 11 and Segmented Backgrounds, Fig. 2-5 on page 17.)

The sky is colored a very light blue at the horizon, graduating to a darker blue at the top. The ground is colored a green brown. The flower colors are optional. Yellow and purple were chosen to simulate an autumn scene.

Review Assembly Drawing, Fig. 6.20-2 to familiarize yourself with the layers. The fence post, like the cattails, is made of two glued layers with

Cut out and wood-burn all details on the birds and flowers, and other patterns. (See Figs. 6.20-4 through 6.20-6 on pages 152–154.)

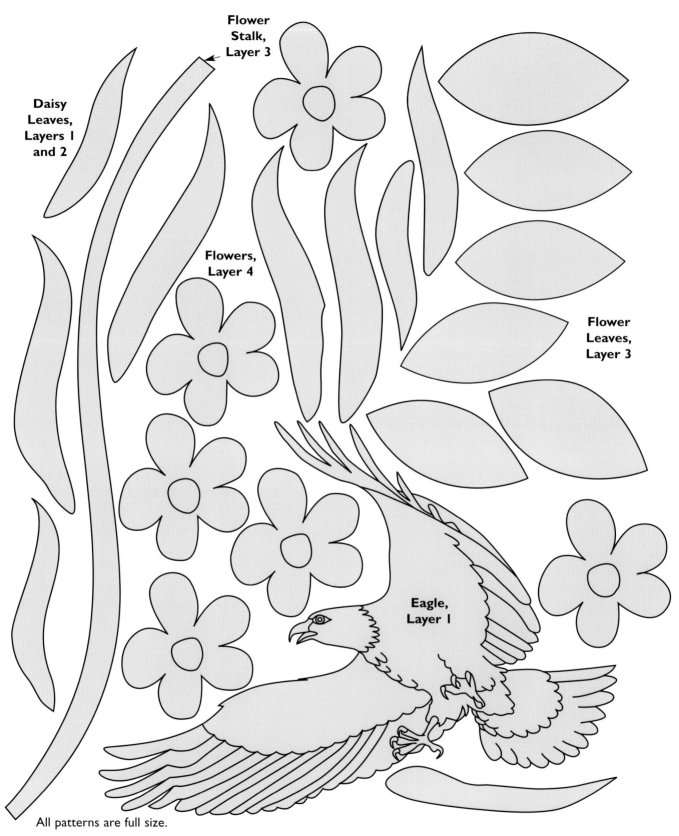

Flower
Stalk,
Layer 3

Daisy
Leaves,
Layers 1
and 2

Flowers,
Layer 4

Flower
Leaves,
Layer 3

Eagle,
Layer 1

All patterns are full size.

Fig. 6.20-4: Fall Pheasants Patterns.

**Daisies,
Layer 1**

**Pheasant,
Layer 4**

**Pheasant,
Layer 3**

Enlarge all patterns 200%.

Fig. 6.20-5: Fall Pheasants Patterns.

153

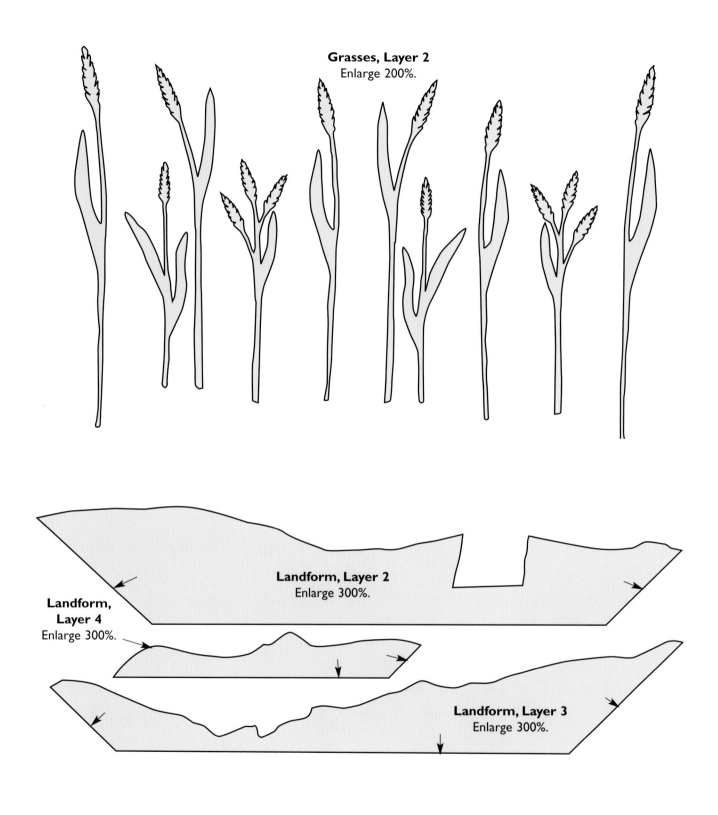

Grasses, Layer 2
Enlarge 200%.

Landform, Layer 2
Enlarge 300%.

**Landform,
Layer 4**
Enlarge 300%.

Landform, Layer 3
Enlarge 300%.

Fig. 6.20-6: Fall Pheasants Patterns. Arrows indicate visible edges that must fit against frame.

154

Coloring the Pheasants. Well-burned feather detailing adds color as well as texture. The female is basically marker-stained a two-tone brown. (See Figs. 6.20-7 and 6.20-8.)

Fig. 6.20-7: Brown of the female nearly complete.

Fig. 6.20-8: Completed female pheasant.

The male requires color blending in the chest and belly areas. Testing of this blended color technique first on scrap is strongly recommended. (See Fig. 6.20-9.)

Fig. 6.20-9: Blended colors of the belly and chest of the male.

Apply a yellow-gold color to this area first. Add some red to the upper chest and blend downward toward the middle of the chest, creating a new color in the blended area. All other areas are straight from the marker colors. The eagle is essentially two different tones of dark gray.

Assembly. The placement of the Layer 1 pieces of the post, daisies, and grasses is best done using the pieces of Layer 2 to help position them. Assure that attention is given to making the key fits of those edges of the landforms identified on the patterns with small arrows. Use shims under Layer 2 and under the eagle. (See Figs. 6.20-10 and 6.20-11 on page 156.)

Fig. 6.20-10: Daisies and four leaves are glued directly to the background.

Fig. 6.20-11: Close-up showing more than ½ of the grass pieces are glued directly to the background.

METRIC EQUIVALENCY CHART

mm-millimeters cm-centimeters
inches to millimeters and centimeters

inches	mm	cm	inches	cm	inches	cm
⅛	3	0.3	9	22.9	30	76.2
¼	6	0.6	10	25.4	31	78.7
½	13	1.3	12	30.5	33	83.8
⅝	16	1.6	13	33.0	34	86.4
¾	19	1.9	14	35.6	35	88.9
⅞	22	2.2	15	38.1	36	91.4
1	25	2.5	16	40.6	37	94.0
1¼	32	3.2	17	43.2	38	96.5
1½	38	3.8	18	45.7	39	99.1
1¾	44	4.4	19	48.3	40	101.6
2	51	5.1	20	50.8	41	104.1
2½	64	6.4	21	53.3	42	106.7
3	76	7.6	22	55.9	43	109.2
3½	89	8.9	23	58.4	44	111.8
4	102	10.2	24	61.0	45	114.3
4½	114	11.4	25	63.5	46	116.8
5	127	12.7	26	66.0	47	119.4
6	152	15.2	27	68.6	48	121.9
7	178	17.8	28	71.1	49	124.5
8	203	20.3	29	73.7	50	127.0

yards to meters

yards	meters	yards	meters	yards	meters	yards	meters	yards	meters
⅛	0.11	2⅛	1.94	4⅛	3.77	6⅛	5.60	8⅛	7.43
¼	0.23	2¼	2.06	4¼	3.89	6¼	5.72	8¼	7.54
⅜	0.34	2⅜	2.17	4⅜	4.00	6⅜	5.83	8⅜	7.66
½	0.46	2½	2.29	4½	4.11	6½	5.94	8½	7.77
⅝	0.57	2⅝	2.40	4⅝	4.23	6⅝	6.06	8⅝	7.89
¾	0.69	2¾	2.51	4¾	4.34	6¾	6.17	8¾	8.00
⅞	0.80	2⅞	2.63	4⅞	4.46	6⅞	6.29	8⅞	8.12
1	0.91	3	2.74	5	4.57	7	6.40	9	8.23
1⅛	1.03	3⅛	2.86	5⅛	4.69	7⅛	6.52	9⅛	8.34
1¼	1.14	3¼	2.97	5¼	4.80	7¼	6.63	9¼	8.46
1⅜	1.26	3⅜	3.09	5⅜	4.91	7⅜	6.74	9⅜	8.57
1½	1.37	3½	3.20	5½	5.03	7½	6.86	9½	8.69
1⅝	1.49	3⅝	3.31	5⅝	5.14	7⅝	6.97	9⅝	8.80
1¾	1.60	3¾	3.43	5¾	5.26	7¾	7.09	9¾	8.92
1⅞	1.71	3⅞	3.54	5⅞	5.37	7⅞	7.20	9⅞	9.03
2	1.83	4	3.66	6	5.49	8	7.32	10	9.14

ABOUT THE AUTHORS

PATRICK SPIELMAN is the world's leading wood-working author, with over 75 books published, including the best-selling *The New Router Handbook* and *Scroll Saw Pattern Book*, which have each sold over one million copies. *The New Router Handbook* won the National Association of Home and Workshop Writers award for Best How-To Book in 1994. A graduate of the University of Wisconsin-Stout, he has taught high school and vocational wood-working in Wisconsin schools for 27 years.

Patrick, with the assistance of his family, owned and operated a wood product manufacturing company for 20 years. Most recently, he published and distributed *Home Workshop News*, a bimonthly newsletter/magazine dedicated to scroll-sawing. Patrick and his wife Patricia own Spielman's Wood Works and Spielman's Kid Works, two gift galleries located in northeastern Wisconsin that feature quality wood products.

Over the course of Patrick's teaching and wood-working careers, he has invented hundreds of jigs, fixtures, and woodworking aids. He has served as a technical consultant and designer for a major tool manufacturer and he continues to pioneer new and exciting techniques for wood-workers as he has done for more than 45 years.

ROBERT HYDE was born and raised in Green Bay, Wisconsin. He began wood-working 25 years ago after he and his wife, Carole, built a house with extensive wall space that needed to be decorated.

He started by adapting stained glass patterns for wood. They looked like two dimensional puzzles and were much harder to make than he expected. In searching for an easier construction process, he decided to layer the individual pieces, which he found much easier than making the exact fit for each piece. Everything grew from there. He added colors and wood-burned details to his pictures to increase their appeal. At the suggestion of a friend, he tried selling them at local craft shows. With Carole's help, this experiment exploded into a full time business. After three years, they were selling 700 pictures a year at craft shows and through consignment at retail shops in Wisconsin and Illinois. They found it to be a lot of time, a lot of work, and a lot of fun.

Five years ago, Robert and Carole retired to their lake home in northern Wisconsin. Robert still makes some wood-working pieces to sell locally, but enjoys having more time to explore variations and to be creative with new ideas.

Index